SPS 8

95¢

THE
SOCIAL BACKGROUND
OF POLITICAL
DECISION-MAKERS

DONALD R. MATTHEWS
Smith College

ed Nations

OUBLEDAY SHORT STUDIES
N POLITICAL SCIENCE

Doubleday Short Studies in Political Science

The Social Background of Political Decision-Makers

By DONALD R. MATTHEWS

Smith College

DOUBLEDAY & COMPANY, INC.

Garden City, N.Y.

1954

LIBRARY OF CONGRESS CATALOG CARD NUMBER 54-10200
PRINTED IN THE UNITED STATES OF AMERICA
AT THE COUNTRY LIFE PRESS, GARDEN CITY, N.Y.

48889

Editor's Foreword

For many centuries, students of government and politics have recognized the key importance of the social foundations of political life. Down through the history of political theory, most classical writers have made at least some allusion to the general relationships between political institutions on the one hand and the structure of society on the other. In particular, considerable attention has been paid to the possible connections between social stratification and political power. Explicitly and implicitly, this attention can be seen clearly in Aristotle's *Politics*, Plato's *Republic*, in the *Federalist Papers*, and in the writings of Karl Marx; and in the latter-day ideologies which have appeared in the social movements of fascism, communism, and socialism. Within the complex, intertwined American political tradition, the names of Jefferson, Hamilton, Madison, Marshall, Jackson, Webster, Calhoun, Sumner, Ward, Brandeis, Holmes, Bellamy, and many others, suggest how much importance has been attached to the reciprocal impact of the social condition of man and the machinery and processes of government.

Not only influential makers of political theories and traditions, but also outstanding professional students of politics such as Harold Laski, Arthur F. Bentley, Sir Ernest Barker, George Catlin, Charles Beard, Charles Merriam, and Harold Lasswell pioneered in the effort to build into the main body of political science some of the cumulative observations and interpretations of social factors relevant to systematic political analysis.

Despite the sustained interest and substantial contribution on the part of scholars and active participants in politics, the treatment of social factors has tended to remain fragmentary and largely intuitive until quite recently. One can be grateful for the data and insights of the great minds of the past and yet realize that there are unfortunate gaps in our knowledge. For example, with respect to the social origins of those who achieve political power in the United States, studies of Pendleton Herring (*Federal Commissioners*, 1936) and McKinney (see articles cited in the footnotes to this study) still stand out among those contributed by political scientists. Much of the writing on the social backgrounds of politics has been by sociologists who may or may not be known to most present-day teachers and students of political science—Pareto, Mosca, Mannheim, Weber, and Durkheim.

More recently, social scientists have shown renewed interest in broadening the base of political analysis. This has been due in part to the desire of political scientists to probe the "dynamic," "informal," and "human" factors of formal governmental institutions and to answer the "why" questions of political action. These developments are at once typified by, and embodied in, the following: S. M. Lipset and R. Bendix, *Class, Status and Power*; Louis Kesselman, *The Social Politics of F.E.P.C.*; David Riesman, *The Lonely Crowd*; Floyd Hunter, *Community Power Structure: A Study of Decision-makers*;

David Truman, *The Governmental Process*; C. Wright Mills, *The New Men of Power*; and the Stanford Elite studies.

Professor Matthews' perceptive and compact analytical survey of the social background of political decision-makers is a most welcome addition to the new Doubleday Short Studies in Political Science series. His well-organized summary and interpretation of theories and empirical findings constitute a long-needed unifying and illuminating essay because efforts to explore the significant links between the social origins and behavior of political leaders have not been systematic or comprehensive. Furthermore, the existing scholarly materials bearing on this aspect of socio-political analysis have been widely scattered in the literature.

This study begins by directing the reader's attention to a focus, namely, those individuals who make the political decisions for a society. It is one of the enduring tasks of political science to explain why decision-makers behave as they do. One type of explanation is to be sought, of course, in the possible effects of the decision-maker's social conditioning *before* he takes office. The author takes pains to suggest what is to be learned from an investigation of this subject and why it is important—a highly useful practice often neglected.

Does the decision-maker's socio-economic status and previous life experience make any difference in the way he looks at policy problems? in the social groups he will listen to and agree with? Are certain strata of the population over-represented or under-represented because decision-makers do or do not share their basic characteristics? What kinds of people enter politics? What kinds are predominantly successful? Are everyone's chances of a political career roughly equal? Are decision-makers recruited from all citizens who have the requisite ability, or are some excluded? Is the balance of power and influence among various groups reflected in the social composition of the decision-makers? Do the most high-ranking social groups dominate the decision-maker roles? Does the social status of the government official have anything to do with who has access to him?

Most of us will agree that these are among the crucial questions to be answered by political scientists. It will also be agreed that these are very difficult questions. As noted, classical thinkers and professional scholars have been grappling with them for centuries. Professor Matthews' major contribution is twofold: first, to review briefly but systematically the hypotheses advanced by certain outstanding modern theorists who have attempted to find satisfactory answers to the foregoing questions; second, to summarize the results of factual studies which have a bearing on the theories reviewed. Thus theory and fact are juxtaposed, and the reader is able to see which hypotheses remain untested, which have been tentatively verified and which have not. The author provides an accounting of what we know and what we do not know about the social origins of decision-makers and their consequences for decision-making behavior.

Though it is by no means easy, Professor Matthews has also offered his critical evaluation of both the theories and empirical investigations. In itself, this is a valuable service for we should be reminded of the pitfalls involved in this kind of analysis and of the necessity to decide what data are required and how such data can most effectively be gathered. It is to be noted that included in the factual studies reported are the author's own original researches on American senators.

The reader will notice that certain larger issues are raised and discussed throughout. First, what light, if any, is cast by the empirical findings on the concept of the ruling class or classes? Does social stratification inevitably lead to class domination? Second, what is the relationship between the form of government and the kind of people who are recruited to political office? Does a democracy necessarily draw its decision-makers from a broader social base than a dictatorship? Third, what are the implications for democratic values and beliefs in the United States of the research on American decision-makers? Are members of Congress a "representative" group of Americans? Is the belief in equality of political opportunity a sentimental illusion? Fourth, what difference does the size of the social base from which decision-makers are chosen make? What losses, if any, result from a narrower base?

Such issues can now be examined in terms of existing materials based on the social background of political leaders in the United States, Great Britain, Germany, and the Soviet Union. The findings so far are by no means conclusive, but when carefully marshalled and put in an interpretive framework, they are imposing and useful.

RICHARD C. SNYDER

Preface

The purpose of this Short Study is to provide a brief analysis of the theoretical writings and factual studies about the social and psychological backgrounds of government officials.

Considerable work has been done on this subject by political scientists, sociologists and psychologists. While the books and articles on the subject are numerous, they are widely scattered and have been written by scholars with different interests, assumptions and vocabularies. For some time it has seemed to me that if these facts and ideas could be drawn together some new insights and general conclusions of interest to students of politics might emerge. The following pages represent my efforts to perform this task. I will be both delighted and surprised if all the readers of this Short Study agree with the approach I have taken and the conclusions I have drawn. But I will be satisfied if this attempt at integration helps some readers make sense out of a multitude of facts and ideas.

The large quantity of literature on political decision-makers which provides this study with its *raison d'être* has also imposed limitations upon it. What follows is, of necessity, severely selective. I have tried to discuss, compare and evaluate only those studies which I consider to be theoretically relevant to an understanding of politics. The justification of this approach is presented at some length in Chapter Two. The scope of the study was also determined in large measure by the existence of adequate studies made by others. Thus in Chapters Three and Four I have confined my attention to the political leaders of the United States, Great Britain, Germany and the Soviet Union and ignored those of other nations about which less is known. The title of this book, like so many others, really should be prefaced by the words, "Some Aspects of. . . ." The rather extensive notes which may be found at the end of this volume are not intended (to rephrase Veblen) as symbols of "conspicuous scholarship" but as a stimulus and guide to those readers who choose to pursue the subject further than I have been able to here.

I am indebted to the University of Chicago and to W. W. Norton and Company, for permission to quote at length from copyrighted material. Portions of this work appeared in the *Public Opinion Quarterly*, Vol. 18 (1954), and is used here with the Editor's permission.

Finally, I want to take this opportunity to thank Professor Richard C. Snyder for his encouragement and advice during the preparation of this manuscript. His contribution to this work has been exceeded only by that made by my wife, to whom I owe my greatest debt. Despite all this assistance, I have no doubt made errors of fact and judgment for which I accept full responsibility.

May 1954
Northampton, Mass.

DONALD R. MATTHEWS

Contents

chapter one

Why Study Social Backgrounds?

The essence of government is the act of choice, the making of decisions. Most of these decisions are on relatively unimportant questions. Can a city afford to repave Main Street this year? How can nearly extinct bird species be best protected? Are the advertisements of a specific patent medicine firm misleading? Should the field service of a federal department have its offices in state capitals? Questions of this sort may be of great interest to a few people or groups, yet decisions made on them have little impact on the day-to-day life of the average citizen. But modern governments are also called upon to make decisions of tremendous importance, decisions that have consequences felt by millions of people. For example, how can the Taft-Hartley Act be modified to meet the demands of management and organized labor as well as the interests of the other members of the community? If these conflicting wants and needs cannot be simultaneously achieved, which should give way and how much? Or, to take another area of political controversy, how much money must be spent on military forces to achieve adequate security from Soviet aggression? What after all is adequate security? How can the desire for national security be reconciled with other values and wants such as individual freedom, a stable economy, lower taxes? Do we need a balanced military force and substantial strength in conventional weapons, or should the United States rely heavily upon atomic and hydrogen bombs and the long-range airplanes to deliver them? It seems unnecessary to continue illustrating the complexity and importance of many governmental problems—a glance at today's newspaper will supply many more examples.

Politics and Decision-Making

Important political decisions such as these are made in a variety of ways in different nations. In some, major political decisions are made by a handful of men possessing nearly absolute power and unrestrained by law or by a sense of public responsibility. In the case of the United States and other modern democracies, major political decisions are made by a far larger group of men, many of whom are popularly elected and all of whom are subject to constitutional law and to varying degrees of self-restraint imposed by a sense of responsibility to the community. Consequently under democratic conditions the discretion of the decision-maker is severely circumscribed by public opinion, law, custom, and self-restraint in the form of values brought to official duties by the individual decision-maker. In modern dictatorships, on the other hand, the restrictions on the choices of the decision-makers from such sources are much less narrow. Despite the wide variety of ways in which important political decisions are made, they are *always* and *everywhere* made by a relatively few men acting as public officials. It is this limited group of public officials, here called *decision-makers*, who are the subject of this study.

In their efforts to understand political decision-making, political scientists have emphasized the study of institutions rather than the study of men. Countless studies have been made of the Presidency, Congress, courts, and political parties; but only a handful have been devoted to Presidents, Congressmen, judges, and politicians. Of course institutional analyses ultimately are concerned with human behavior, but the institutional approach places such an emphasis on formal, prescribed relationships and rules of behavior—on what *should* happen—that what *does* happen and *why* is often obscured. "The standard procedure . . . [has been] . . . to take the legal formalities as the theme and to treat everything else as variation."[1] This approach provides only a partial view of political reality. Important political decisions are made by men interacting *within* an institutional context. It is the basic premise of this study that the social and psychological characteristics of the individual officials acting within a political institutional framework must be considered before an adequate understanding of politics and government is possible.

Social Background of Political Decision-Makers

This study is an attempt to contribute to a more complete view of political decision-making by analyzing the social backgrounds of political decision-makers. What insights into politics can this approach yield? How can this kind of research lead to a more reliable explanation and enhanced understanding of political phenomena? It seems to the author that this approach can make three principal contributions to political science.

Human Factors in the Analysis of Political Decision-Making

The participants in political struggles are not ciphers; they are ". . . not equivalent to the steel ball in a pinball game, bumping passively from post to post down an inclined plane."[2] They are complicated human beings. They bring with them into the political arena their own set of particular individual interests, biases, and predispositions. James Madison saw this when he wrote:

No man is allowed to be judge in his own cause, because his interest would certainly bias his judgment, and, not improbably, corrupt his integrity. With equal, nay with even greater reason, a body of men are unfit to be both judges and parties at the same time; yet what are many of the most important acts of legislation, but so many judicial determinations, not indeed concerning the rights of single persons, but concerning the rights of large bodies of citizens? And what are the different classes of legislators but advocates and parties to the causes which they determine?[3]

The conviction that the political decision-maker's behavior and decisions are influenced by his personal life experiences not only has a long and honorable history but also is substantiated by modern psychological and sociological research. We are told that human beings are selective in what they perceive, or experience through their senses, and that identical events or facts have different meanings for different people.[4] For example, two people see the same Negro asleep under the same shade tree: one may interpret this to mean that all Negroes are lazy and shiftless, while the other may conclude that Negro

housing conditions are intolerable. Or, if the two observers are a lumberman
and a botanist, they may not be aware of the drowsing Negro at all; the lumberman sees only the salable lumber in the tree, the botanist sees the tree as
a member of an unusual botanical family.

Human beings perceive what goes on about them within a *frame of reference*
determined by their total previous experiences. The world that we experience
is not just "given," it is influenced by what our parents taught us as children,
by our friendships and group memberships, our occupations, our formal education, and so on. We thus obtain a directional guide that focuses our attention on those things which fit into established patterns of thought and filters
out experiences which do not. In a similar fashion we develop tendencies,
called *attitudes*, to react in a certain way to stimuli.

Frames of reference and attitudes are of course heavily influenced by the
dominant values and beliefs of the society in which a person lives. But the
frames of reference and attitudes of members of the same society vary considerably. Each belongs to or identifies himself with different groups; each
has different experiences and a different life history. Identical events will take
on different meanings and will therefore result in differing behavior.

It is easy to see the influence of frames of reference and attitudes in simpli-
fied situations. What is significant to this study is that similar processes take
place under more complex conditions. Consider, for example, the United
States Congressman.[5] First of all, he may within limits decide for himself just
what his job involves. Should he literally *represent* the interests and opinions
of his constituents, or should he (in cases of conflict) vote on the basis of his
own personal evaluation of the merits of an issue? When the Congressman
decides "to vote his conscience," his personal attitudes are of obvious importance. But when he decides that "the time has come to rise above conscience," his estimate of the situation will be influenced by his attitudes and
frame of reference. A rational calculation of electoral forces back home is a
difficult task at best. When time is short and political information and advice
conflict, it seems likely that the Congressman often will see what he wants
to see and conclude that his opinions and the opinions of his constituents
are pretty much the same. Similarly the Congressman's motivations, his competence at political manipulation, his accessibility to political interest groups,
and the impact of his thought and action, all are influenced by his total life
experience. For reasons such as these one recent student of the American
legislative process suggests that the beliefs and preferences built into the
Congressman's personality through socialization, education, and previous experience are often more important in determining his vote than the overt
pressures from political interest groups. And, he adds, ". . . by and large, the
basic social philosophy of a legislator is set before he comes to Congress. It is
for this reason that the study of a legislator from the Washington perspective
alone is bound to be one-dimensional."[6]

Thus it is plain that a consideration of the human factors adds a new dimen-
sion to the analysis of political decision-making. Political scientists must take
into account the attitudes and frames of reference of the men who are legislators, judges, presidents, and prime ministers. This is not to deny of course
that organizational factors and legal or customary rules do not also influence
the behavior of decision-makers. Nor does this analysis deny that political
decision-makers in democracies are under great pressure to conform to public

opinion. It is suggested, however, that all these factors are perceived, interpreted, and given meaning by individual mental processes and that these processes are heavily inflenced by the individual's previous experience. The study of the social backgrounds of political decision-makers thus contributes to a deeper understanding of the actions and decisions of those in positions of political authority.

Recruitment of Decision-Makers

Who should rule? On the basis of what principle of selectivity should political decision-makers be chosen? These have been among the basic questions of all time. The history of political thought has been in large part the history of man's attempt to find acceptable answers to them. These are not "merely theoretical" questions. Rather they are highly practical ones. Every political system must contain some institutionalized means of recruiting decision-makers if it is to endure. It is no accident that so much of the attention of students of government has been devoted to the problem. How can the study of social characteristics and career patterns of political decision-makers contribute to an understanding of why recruitment arrangements function as they do?

First and foremost, the establishment of institutional machinery calculated to gain a given objective does not by any means insure its realization. For example, as far as institutions go, the American system of selecting public officials through popular election is intended to be and appears to be democratic. But does this system promote the development and actual recruitment of competent political decision-makers? Are opportunities to hold public office roughly equal for all members of American society? Popular stereotypes lead one to suspect that America's most talented men do not enter politics.[7] Is this true? If so, why? What are the blocks to political advancement in the United States? If there are substantial barriers, what can be done to achieve greater equality of political opportunity?

In order to answer questions of this sort a far broader and less formalistic conception of the selection process is needed. Who becomes a political decision-maker is not just decided by elections, primaries, and voting but rather is also the result of a continual sifting and sorting of the citizens who enter the quest for political power. By conventional devices and practices, societies set up barriers to political advancement for some and encourage others. The way in which this social selection is done and the bases and criteria of elimination have considerable impact on the competence of persons who become political decision-makers. Certainly these subtle processes may eliminate a far larger number of potential decision-makers than do primaries and elections; and the continued existence and efficient operation of a political system depends upon the development and attraction of competent political decision-makers.

Decision-Makers and Social Change

There is a third and final reason for studying the backgrounds of these men. Changes in their social background may be an indication of over-all social and economic change. For instance, look at the differences in the social backgrounds of the top-level personnel in the Roosevelt, Truman, and Eisenhower administrations. The professors and patrician reformers of Roosevelt's day, one journalist suggests, were replaced under Truman by professional politicians, and now ". . . the Eisenhower Revolution has put a wholly new face upon Washington: the face of the businessman in government."[8] Observers of American politics are almost universally agreed that these changes are related to significant differences in the habits of thought and in the policies of the three administrations. Are these changes a *cause* or a *result* of a shifting balance of power in America? America is often characterized as a Business Civilization, yet being governed by so many business leaders is a new experience. Are business leaders no longer content to leave the direction of the state in the hands of sympathetic political agents such as lawyers and professional politicians? If so, why? Or is the sharp change due to the personal whim of a president? Questions like these beg for answers. Careful research and imaginative theorizing about trends in the social backgrounds of political decision-makers may supply some new insight into the phenomena of social and political change.

Summary

There are, therefore, three major ways in which research into the social backgrounds of political decision-makers can aid students of political behavior to develop a more adequate understanding of their subject. This type of study can provide the foundation for a clearer appreciation of the decision-making process and *why* decision-makers decide the way they do. It may make it possible for political scientists to derive a more reliable picture of how decision-makers are selected. It may contribute another perspective to the study of the relationship between social and political change. While such matters hardly exhaust what political scientists want and need to know, the potential contributions of research in this area may be quite substantial.

Although the vast majority of political scientists have shown relatively little interest in this area of study, a small minority of the profession has been doing research in this field for half a century, and there is much evidence that the present trend is toward a greater interest in this type of study. Moreover a fairly large amount of empirical research and a substantial body of theory relating to the subject have been published by members of other academic disciplines, especially sociologists. These studies, however, are widely scattered, and the usual problems of interdisciplinary communication—different interests, assumptions, different terminologies—have diminished their influence among political scientists.

The purpose of this study is to bring some of this material together and in relatively short compass to indicate what is known and what is not known about the social backgrounds of political decision-makers. The time has come to try to sum up and evaluate scattered facts and ideas. Hence in Chapter Two the various theories concerning the social backgrounds of decision-makers will be presented and discussed. In Chapter Three the findings of empirical studies will be summarized and evaluated. Then we shall be in a position for a tentative stock-taking.

chapter two

Some Modern Writers and Their Views

What kind of men become political decision-makers?

This question cannot be answered by the assiduous collection of facts alone. Facts do not speak for themselves. Some kind of theorizing is essential to the development of knowledge. No mortal man can select facts or see their connection or signficance without a theory, a hunch, or an hypothesis.

Research [writes Robert Lynd] without an actively selective point of view becomes the ditty bag of an idiot, filled with bits of pebbles, straws, feathers, and other random hoardings.[1]

In our endeavor to find out the types of men who become political decision-makers, we are not interested in "random hoardings" of unrelated facts. We are concerned that the facts make some sense. This can be done through analysis which selects and orders the facts according to certain criteria.

Therefore the first step in an attempt to answer our question must be to examine the existing theories and hypotheses concerning the social backgrounds of political decision-makers. These theories are concerned with four separate questions:

1. From what social positions are political decision-makers recruited?
2. What are their skills and personality traits?
3. What are the interrelationships between their characteristics and political change or revolution?
4. What are the effects of the characteristics of political decision-makers on the conduct of government?

The remainder of this chapter will be taken up with brief discussion of a number of modern writers' ideas on these four questions. No attempt will be made to analyze the entire body of thought of any of these men. Our attention must of necessity be directed only toward those aspects of their thought relevant to our present inquiry.

Social Position and Political Recruitment

Political decision-makers are more than public officials. They are also members of a society. They belong to social groups such as families, clubs, occupational groups, classes, and churches. They possess many *social positions* or standardized relationships with other people. Most of the theorists in this field suggest that political decision-makers are not recruited from just any group or social position but rather come from relatively few of them.

6

Mosca: The Ruling Class

The first theory, and still one of the most challenging, stressing the political importance of the social position of political decision-makers is Gaetano Mosca's theory of the ruling class. His argument begins with his statement that:

Among the constant facts and tendencies that are to be found in all political organisms, one is so obvious that it is apparent to the most casual eye. In all societies—from societies that are very meagerly developed and have barely attained the dawnings of civilization, down to the most advanced and powerful societies—two classes of people appear—a class that rules and a class that is ruled. The first class, always the less numerous, performs all political functions, monopolizes power and enjoys the advantages that power brings, whereas the second, the more numerous class, is directed and controlled by the first, in a manner that is now more or less legal, now more or less arbitrary and violent . . .[2]

More than just a universal political division of labor is found by Mosca. In addition he says that the political decision-makers inevitably constitute a *class* and that this class inevitably dominates with little or no actual accountability to the mass of the citizenry. Both of these assertions are momentous if true. Let us look at each of these points in turn.

What does Mosca mean by a ruling class? This is not at all clear. At one point his definition appears to be a mere tautology: the ruling class is made up of those who rule. At other points, however, he suggests that the ruling class is the social stratum *from which* the actual rulers are chosen. In either case Mosca suggests that this class will possess a sense of identity and solidarity which results in the class ". . . obeying a single impulse." And he is again quite clear that the ruling class will possess ". . . some attribute, real or apparent, which is highly esteemed and very influential in the society in which they live."[3] For instance, in societies in which warfare is important, the ruling class will be warriors; in societies in which economic aggrandizement is considered important, the ruling class will be the wealthy; and so on. The fact that members of ruling classes are respected and successful people within their respective societies serves as an important claim to legitimacy for ruling minorities, because

. . . ruling classes do not justify their power exclusively be de facto possession of it, but try to find a moral and legal basis for it, representing it as the logical and necessary consequence of doctrines and beliefs that are generally recognized and accepted.[4]

But what does ruling involve? Does it inevitably lead to an uncontrollable domination of the many by the ruling class? Mosca is again found on both sides of the question. While generally he gives the impression that the ruling class possesses ultimate power, he sometimes admits that political pressure from the citizens upon the ruling class is of considerable importance. He also suggests that the ruling class does *not* always "obey a single impulse" and that rivalries within the class will lead to competition for mass political support. When members of the ruling class begin competing for popular support, it can hardly be said that their actions are unaffected by the mass of the citizens.

Thus Mosca is vague and contradictory about what *ruling* involves and what a *class* is; hence a combination of the two concepts into one theory is inevitably confusing. But one feature of his theory demands our attention: is it true, as Mosca argues, that political decision-makers tend to come from highly valued social positions? If so, why? Contemporary theories of stratification suggest answers to both of these questions.

Stratification Theorists: Political Life Chances

Just as some men have dreamed of living without government and law, others have dreamed of living without invidious social distinctions. Neither wish has yet been realized. In all known societies, there exist both a system of government and the ranking of social positions on a scale of superiority and inferiority according to some commonly recognized and accepted basis of valuation.[5] It is this system of ranking that is called *social stratification*.

Individuals and groups may be stratified in many different ways and on many different bases; income, social influence and power, occupation, religion, ethnic origins, and family reputation are familiar bases of social ranking in America, but members of other societies are stratified in quite different ways. It is conceivable that members of a society might be ranked on the basis of such factors as ". . . their emotional stability, their ability to play badminton, their knowledge of medieval Latin, the color of their hair, the number of friends they have, the reputation of their ancestors."[6] Actually relatively few of the possible sources of ranking are used by the members in placing themselves and others in the social hierarchy.

That societies are stratified does not necessarily mean that classes are inevitable. It does mean, however, that individuals filling certain social positions and performing certain activities (or roles) will be considered better than others. But every individual plays many roles, and they may be differently evaluated. In the United States, for example, one and the same individual may be a banker, a member of a relatively low-prestige church, the owner of a new Cadillac, and the son of ignorant and poor immigrants. It is only when an individual's many statuses tend to be regarded as roughly equal for several or all of the criteria of ranking used in a society that relatively stable structures called *classes* or *castes* arise.

The difference between class and caste systems is primarily a difference in the degree of mobility found in the two systems.[7] An individual is born into the Brahman caste in India and always remains in it. In the United States an individual is born into a class (that of his parents) but there is no certainty that he or she will always remain a member of it. In a class system, the adult's social position is based in varying degrees upon his own personal accomplishments as well as other factors. Class and caste systems also differ in the clarity with which the strata are differentiated, the solidarity of the individuals or groups sharing a similar social position, and the magnitude of the invidious distinctions found within the society. In a caste system lines of demarcation are clearly drawn, individuals are very conscious of their caste membership, and the differences in prestige found within the society may be extremely large. In a class system, on the other hand, class boundaries may be vague, and even the actual number of classes may be in doubt. There may be very little class consciousness, and individuals may identify themselves with some other class than the one that others place them in. Finally differences in prestige from the top to the bottom of the society may not be very great. But even in a relatively fluid class system an individual's social status makes a great difference in how he behaves, what he thinks, and what his opportunities are. On this point the evidence is overwhelming.

What has this to do with political personnel? The answer is that the position of top-level political decision-maker is among the most highly valued in contemporary societies.[8] It is at least logically possible that the men who fill these positions might possess differently ranked nonpolitical roles. The local garbage collector, for example, might also be the mayor. But the ideas of Mosca, as well as those of other thinkers,[9] suggest that this will not normally occur. In societies with class or caste systems those individuals who become important political decision-makers will usually also possess highly valued social positions. For example, it will be more common for mayors to be lawyers or businessmen than manual laborers.

This is not really a surprising hypothesis. When a system of stratification is generally accepted, one must expect the people to look up to those near the top of it as unusually worthy and talented individuals capable of grappling with the political problems of the day. This may not in fact always be true. The skills and ability needed to become socially successful may not be the same as those needed in politics. But those who meet a society's definition of social success benefit from a halo effect nonetheless.

While these ideas are certainly influenced by Mosca's analysis of the so-called ruling class, it should be noted that they are rather far removed from Mosca's "elitist" conclusions. Contemporary stratification theory suggests only that under stable conditions political decision-makers normally will be chosen from among those with the most prestige in a community. However stratification analysis does not suggest that *all* political decision-makers will be chosen from one class, nor that they will consider themselves a self-conscious leadership group, nor that they will inevitably dominate the mass of the citizens. Rather stratification analysis suggests the probability that the political life-chances of those with high social status will be considerably better than those with average or low prestige. In Chapter Three we shall see the extent to which the facts back up this hypothesis.

Personality and Skills

Speculation about political decision-makers has by no means been confined to a consideration of the social positions from which they are drawn. There has been as much, if not more, effort given to determining the effect upon recruitment of their personalities and skills.

Timasheff: Natural Leaders

From earliest times writers have assumed that there are natural leaders especially equiped by personality or skill to perform important political roles. More than two thousand years ago Plato built his ideal city upon the foundation of such an assumption. Machiavelli believed that some men have special "virtue," that is, especially strong desires for power and abilities to be politically successful.

These assumptions are widely shared today. For example, Bertrand Russell in his *Power: A New Social Analysis* writes that the two moving forces in history are the impulse to power and the impulse to submission.

> Some men's characters lead them always to command, others' always to obey; between these extremes lie the mass of average human beings, who like to command in some situations, but in others prefer to be subject to a leader.[10]

A more elaborate theory based on similar assumptions has been presented by N. S. Timasheff. To Timasheff[11] every group is naturally divided into two categories, the active and the passive. This is not in its natural form the result of organizational necessity but the result of individual differences in what he calls "dominance feelings." Under natural conditions the active segment of a group is made up of those with high dominance feelings and the passive segment, of those with low dominance feelings. But in complex societies an *organizational* necessity for a political division of labor arises, and power holders are selected by regularized methods. Thus men may obtain power because they are the oldest sons of monarchs or because they champion popular causes. Then the achievement of power no longer depends solely upon the strength of one's dominance feelings. This introduces an inevitable source of political instability in complex societies, for if too many natural leaders are shunted aside from the path to power by "artificial" (i.e., institutional) barriers, a large number of natural leaders will be frustrated and may resort to force or demagoguery to obtain the share of power which they desire.

Timasheff's highly schematic theory makes one important point and overlooks another. First of all, it suggests that the existence of a large group of persons with strong power drives who are not in positions where these desires may be satisfied are dangerous to political stability. But the theory ignores the possibility that the *desire* for power and the *ability* to use it effectively may not always go together. The difficulty of devising a satisfactory formal system of selecting political leaders flows from the necessity of attempting to satisfy individual power drives as well as from the need for political competence in a world in which these two personal characteristics do not always accompany each other. Certainly this was what Charles Merriam had in mind when he wrote in *Political Power:*

> High up among the causes of morbidity in political society . . . is the failure of the system of selection and succession of the responsible governors, whether one, few, or many . . . The breakdown of the accepted system of selection, or its weak functioning, is the recurring cause of malaise and perhaps destruction of the *status quo* in political power. If the old men display senility instead of sagacity, if the hereditary lion produces an ass, if the electors choose a fool or a demagogue, if the self-selected elite are incompetent and untrustworthy, if the army chieftains produce bravery without might, then the way is open to the sickness of the society.[12]

Pareto: Lions and Foxes

One of the most original and complex theories sharing this point of view was written by Vilfredo Pareto. Like Timasheff, he classifies people into two types, but he classifies them on the basis of their sentiments.[13] One type, the "foxes," possesses what Pareto calls the "instinct of combinations," a special ability for innovation and manipulation. The second type, the "lions," has the opposite characteristics; they are not very clever and are traditionalists and men of faith and force. Both types of men can and do become members of the ruling elite, which Pareto defines as the small group possessing the most power in the community. But an elite dominated exclusively by either personality type cannot preserve political stability. When the foxes are in power, the lions will become enraged at the foxes' clever but amoral scheming. Since they are no match for the foxes in political manipulation, the lions will resort to violence in their efforts to overthrow the regime. Once the lions dominate, however, they will discover that men cannot rule by coercion alone. The result of this condition is then a perpetual "circulation of the elite." At different stages in this cycle those possessing the two personality types have differing chances of becoming elite members. Yet if this circulation stops (Pareto believes that elite members will try to maintain their dominant position) then political instability is the inevitable result. The actual decision-makers and the relative importance of the two personality types among decision-makers must change to meet changing conditions.

Lasswell: The Political Personality

Of contemporary political analysts few have been more stimulating and fruitful than Harold Lasswell. The center of his thought is his theory of the "political personality." According to Lasswell, a political personality is characterized by ". . . the accentuation of power in relation to other values within the personality when compared with other persons."[14] In other words, the politician differs from others in placing an abnormally high value on obtaining power.

All members of a society carry out many different roles and they may place quite different emphasis upon them. For example, some may consider their family roles more important than their occupational roles, or vice versa. While the scales of priorities of members of the same society tend to be similar, there are substantial variations. In a society in which political activities are not highly valued by most people, those who seek power are atypical, abnormal in this respect at least. But why are some people motivated to seek power? The Lasswellian analysis suggests a number of reasons. First of all, it may be a very rational adjustment to one's social position. For example, many immigrants and sons of immigrants in the United States, finding that many channels of upward mobility are closed to them, enter machine politics where their foreign names and backgrounds may actually be an advantage in their striving for success.[15] Others may seek power as a means to some other end: wealth, self-satisfaction, security, and so on. But the power drive, according to Lasswell, is also explicable in psychological terms. The political personality, with its preoccupation with the attainment of power, may also be the result of an individual's "ungratified craving for deference." These cravings, unsatisfied in private life, are satisfied by seeking and obtaining power, the gratifications thus obtained compensating for the power-seeker's low estimate of himself. Yet it seems likely that there are other ways of sublimating the unsatisfied need for deference. Why do some make a political solution to their psychological problems while others do not? This depends on the individual's political opportunities and skills. Thus Lasswell suggests a way in which the factors of social structure (which determines political opportunities), personality structure (which supplies the political motivation), and skills (which determine the level of political success) might be combined into a single unified theory of political decision-makers. At least it seems likely that an adequate answer to the question of who becomes a political decision-maker will have to include all three of these factors.

Social Change, Revolution, and Decision-Makers

The theories analyzed so far have tried to answer questions about the social position, personality, and skills of political decision-makers in all stable and enduring political systems. An exclusive concern for these questions is likely to be unrealistic. First of all, theories which attempt to explain the common characteristics of all stable political regimes are of necessity highly abstract. In order to develop generalizations about political decision-makers equally true in China, the United States, the Soviet Union, and the Trobriand Islands, one must overlook vast differences in detail for the few basic similarities. Thus at times these high-level generalizations seem rather far removed from the mundane world of politics. Less abstract generalizations which make no claims to universality but are concerned with developments in a limited number of situations are certain to be more concrete and probably more useful for purposes of empirical analysis.[16] Second, the theories considered so far have been concerned primarily with stable societies; yet if anything is constant, it is the fact of social and political change. Thus in this section we shall examine the less abstract theories which attempt to point up and explain the relationship between social and political change and the characteristics of political decision-makers.

Burnham: The Managerial Revolution

James Burnham thinks he knows how the major economic change of modern times, the industrial revolution, has influenced political decision-making. Burnham's thesis can be briefly summarized:

. . . no individual produces, by himself, everything that he uses; in our society most people produce, by themselves, hardly anything. The production is a social process.
[Therefore]
The instruments of economic production are, simply, the means whereby men live. In any society, the group of persons controlling these means is by that very fact socially dominant.
[Thus it follows that]
Where there is such a controlling group in society, a group which, as against the rest of society, has a greater measure of control over the access to the instruments of production and a preferential treatment in the distribution of the products of those instruments, we may speak of this group as the socially dominant or ruling class in that society.[17]

Members of this group, once individual entrepreneurs and the owners of industry, are rapidly becoming the managers of industry. Since administrators are rapidly taking over control of governments as well as corporations, the ultimate triumph of the managerial class will be the moment when industry is nationalized. Then even the minimal control exercised over the managers by the legal owners of industry will be destroyed, and the bureaucrats will be in total control of the society, its economy, and its government. "The state . . .

will, if we wish to put it that way, be the 'property' of the managers. And that will be quite enough to place them in the position of ruling class."[18]

The events of the last thirty years or so certainly give this theory an air of plausibility, yet it seems to be open to serious challenge. At first glance Burnham's theory of the managerial revolution seems to be based on an essentially Marxist idea: that people with the same relationship to the process of production will constitute a self-conscious class. But Burnham's error is even greater than Marx's, for he defines "managers" on the basis of work-technique rather than on a relationship to the productive process. Administrators in the Bureau of the Budget, General Motors, the NAM, Farmers' Union, CIO, and the Army Engineers are all "managers" by definition;[19] yet they do not have the same relationship to the process of production. Obviously there are vast conflicts of interest within the managerial group when it is defined so broadly. The managers in the Bureau of the Budget benefit from the expansion of government power and activities. Those in the NAM lose. The "pork-choppers" in the CIO work for higher wages and greater benefits for the organization's members: the managers of General Motors are likely to be fired if the CIO is too successful. And few sharper clashes can be found than those between the fellow bureaucrats in the Army Engineers and the Bureau of Reclamation. Until such conflicts between competing sets of managers cease (and as long as the term *manager* is defined so broadly this seems unlikely), it is highly unrealistic to consider managers as constituting a self-conscious and homogeneous class.

But perhaps group solidarity is an unnecessary part of the thesis of the managerial revolution. Perhaps managers will enjoy ultimate power despite their failure to identify themselves with other managers. If by this it is meant that a political division of labor is necessary in voluntary associations, labor unions, and corporations as well as in government, this is true. If, however, this statement is interpreted to mean that these managers will inevitably dominate in an irresponsible and uncontrollable way, it is not true. For as long as there are conflicts of interest within the managerial group, the unavoidable temptation will always exist for one segment (for example, union leaders) to appeal for popular support in their conflict with other managers (say, corporate management). Once the process of competitive bidding for popular support has begun in this fashion, the power of the managers is no longer absolute. It has become contingent upon popular approval.

Burnham's theory of the managerial revolution also suffers from a far too facile translation of control over business decisions and corporate property into control over the state. No competent observer would deny that control over large aggregates of corporate wealth gives certain individuals a great deal of potential political power. But control over the means of production does not equal control over the state despite Marx and despite Burnham. If it did, recent political history would have to be rewritten. The gradual trend in democratic countries toward more government welfare programs and the curbing of the excesses of private business by government action were opposed by the vast majority of those who control corporate power. Yet mass voting power was able to win through despite this opposition.

Probably the most vulnerable aspect of Burnham's theory of the managerial revolution is that it is an exaggeration of an essentially valid observation. Managers are more powerful in a world of big business and big labor and big government than in a world of farmers, small businessmen, competitive markets, and inactive government. But to generalize this into inevitable domination of society by these managers is unjustifiable without presenting supporting reasons. And Burnham's principal "reasons" do not stand up to careful analysis.

Mannheim: Industrialism and Rationality

Another theorist, Karl Mannheim, has explained in a quite different way the impact of industrialism on the characteristics of political decision-makers.[20] While his conclusions are almost as gloomy as Burnham's, his arguments are by no means similar.

The most important result of the industrial revolution according to Mannheim has been the centralization of decision-making. Economic decisions once made by thousands of small entrepreneurs and farmers now are made by a relatively few corporate managers. Political decisions which used to be made by a myriad of local officials now are made centrally by national governments, and especially by their executives. The result of this centralization of decision-making has been an increase of functional rationality (the coordination of means so as to attain most efficiently a given end). But the rise of functional rationality, by its very nature, has deprived the average individual of opportunities to develop individual insight and understanding of complex situations which Mannheim calls substantial rationality. The independent craftsman, for example, exercised both functional and substantial rationality. He not only had to decide how to make his product efficiently but also had to determine its design, the quantity and quality to produce, and so on. Today the factory worker uses his reason in the more limited sense of deciding the most efficient way to perform a given task. Decisions calling for the use of substantial rationality are made by a small managing minority of the society.

A trend toward political democracy has gone along with this trend toward a decline in the exercise of substantial rationality by the many. Political democracy develops competent leadership in its early period, Mannheim argues, because, despite the democratic ideology, political leaders are still chosen from a very small class of propertied and educated men. As this exclusiveness of the old ruling class breaks down in the face of democratic demands, and as more ordinary men become acceptable as political leaders, two things happen. First, political leaders chosen from the lower strata of society will usually have little experience in and aptitude for the use of substantial rationality. Thus modern democracies open ". . . the door to irrationalities in those places where rational direction is indispensable."[21] Second, since the independent judgments of the vast majority are in a state of atrophy, irrationality will become politically popular, and a longing and demand for a Leader will become irresistible. Modern industrialism, by concentrating substantial rationality into the hands of a few and by destroying the fabric of the old status-conscious society, is likely to destroy democracy.

Note how Mannheim's theory contrasts with some others we have already analyzed. Mosca and Pareto maintain that the social characteristics of a ruling class must change to meet changing conditions if stability is to be maintained. Mannheim, however, warns that under modern conditions this may not be true; too rapid change may bring irrational leadership and thus disaster. Furthermore, although Mannheim's theory starts with the same observation and ends with a conclusion similar to Burnham's, the two theories are otherwise contradictory. Burnham thinks that the concentration of decision-making stemming from modern industrialism is incompatible with an increase in the political power of the masses, yet it is just this likelihood that frightens Mannheim. There is almost no end to the prophets of doom, but they have yet to agree how or why doom is coming!

Pareto: The Coming of Fascism

Pareto's theory of the circulation of the elite (part of which was summarized on page 10) contains still another view of the relationship between economic change and the characteristics of political decision-makers.[22]

His ideas on this subject begin once again with the distinction between individuals possessing "instincts of combinations" (innovators, manipulators, i.e. foxes) and those possessing "persistence of aggregates" (traditionalists, men of force and faith, i.e. lions). Individuals possessing the two classes of sentiments have different economic as well as political behavior patterns. Speculators are the economic counterparts to the foxes. The economic equivalent of the lions are called *rentiers*, i.e., cautious, orthodox, and thrifty people. With the rise of the foxes to political power, according to Pareto, comes the economic predominance of speculators. The manipulative skills of the speculators as well as their freedom from the bindings of tradition result in a wave of prosperity during the economic and political domination of leaders with a high instinct of combinations. Also during this same period rationalism and skepticism are the dominant modes of thought, and the arts flourish in the atmosphere of liberality. But just as the foxes have fatal flaws for governing, so have the speculators a blind spot for running an economy: they are extravagant. Eventually the speculators are spending more money than the rentiers can save, and the continued prosperity of the nation is threatened. This growing economic menace, when combined with the obvious weakness of the foxes as a ruling class and the growing indignation of the lions and rentiers, results in a violent reaction. The lions take over the control of the state by force, with either the tacit consent or active help of the rentiers. Rationalism and liberality are replaced by an absolute, quasi-religious faith imposed, if need be, by force.

There is little doubt that Pareto intended this scheme, even though expressed in abstract terms, to be a prediction of the immediate future of modern civilization. Democratization and industrialization are the results of rule by the foxes and the speculators. But after this period of relative freedom, prosperity, and liberality will come a period of reaction, extolling the use of force, the blind acceptance of faith, and forced conformity to tradition—in a word, Fascism. But the ultimate cause of this is not impersonal economic forces or mass irrationality but the instability of the personality types and skills of elite members. Thus Pareto adds still another competing interpretation of social, political, and economic change: one in which the nature of a society's leadership is of primary importance.

Lasswell: The World Revolution of Our Time

Harold Lasswell suggests a similar interpretation of the impact of recent social and economic change on the composition and characteristics of political decision-makers.[23]

Three trends are especially significant, according to Lasswell, in understanding the past and possible future of decision-makers: first, the trend toward industrialism and the discovery of new techniques of mass destruction; second, the tendency of world power to become concentrated in the hands of two or three nations; and third, the resulting crisis of world insecurity. As a consequence of these economic, political, and technological changes, decision-makers have changed from men with aristocratic, preindustrial backgrounds to businessmen and their advisers and agents, the lawyers. In the face of continued crisis these men give way to professional politicians, specialists in persuasion and manipulation. But, Lasswell concludes, if the world crisis continues, the specialists in persuasion will give way in ruling circles to the specialists in coercion. These men are of two types, the specialists in the use of violence (military men, political police, etc.) and the specialists in nonviolent coercion (monopolists, managers of monopoly political parties, and bureaucrats in positions that are publicly unaccountable). While Lasswell is the first to admit that this is only one of many possible future developments, he obviously thinks this trend is highly possible and highly ominous. Yet it is the rapid shift in the composition of political elites in this direction along with a corresponding shift in the vocabulary and symbols used by these elites which he considers "the world revolution of our time."

Summary: The Politics of Pessimism

This review of theories about the influence of recent social and economic changes on the characteristics of political decision-makers shows that all are agreed that these changes have had and will continue to have a great impact. They are further agreed that modern conditions place a formidable burden on all political leadership, but especially democratic leadership. Finally all are agreed that modern democracy may not (or in some cases, will not) be able to meet this challenge and that some form of oligarchy is likely (or inevitable) in the future.

Are these conclusions merely a rationalization of their authors' basically antidemocratic attitudes? Certainly some of the theorists considered above were hardly objective, and a few were, as individuals, contemptuous of democratic values. It is unfortunately true that those accepting democratic values, perhaps because of a misguided animosity to authority, have left ". . . to the proponents of authoritarian and aristocratic-conservative politics the elaboration of a political theory of leadership."[24] But is this frequent bias of writers on the subject the only reason for their often antidemocratic conclusions? Or have theorists in this field found some logic in the facts which other writers in the field have ignored? This question now requires our attention.

The Problem of Democracy

Democratic theory, as it pertains to political decision-makers, requires four things: (1) that the decision-makers be competent to perform their duties, (2) that this competence be determined by popular election (for policy makers) or by means of objective tests (for specialists), (3) that competition for positions as political decision-makers be free and that opportunities be open equally to all, and (4) that political decision-makers be accountable and responsive to popular opinion. The pessimists deny that one or all of these conditions can be achieved and say that as a result oligarchy is inevitable.

Is Oligarchy Inevitable?

In their view the political division of labor must under modern conditions and despite democratic political institutions concentrate political power and political competence in the hands of a few.[25] The economic facts of life concentrate power into the hands of managers, according to Burnham; the continual threat of war concentrates power into the hands of the military, according to Lasswell. Moreover, modern life not only increases the number and complexity of political decisions that have to be made, it also concentrates ability to make wise policy decisions. The mass of the citizens are more and more prone to irrational behavior and apathy. When confronted with today's tangle of amazingly complex problems, most people lose interest in public affairs and "privitize" their world. They merely want to be led and are grateful when a leader makes decisions for them. Men in authority are considered both by the masses and by themselves to be indispensable. The leaders tend to use their public authority to perpetuate their position, and this personal concern becomes more important to them than doing their jobs well. The decision-maker's position is still further solidified by the tendency of the people even in a democracy to choose leaders of a higher social status than their own, to want someone to look up to. The struggle for responsible government has been a struggle against the intrusion of the political decision-makers' private interests into the performance of their public jobs. It has also been a struggle to make decision-makers responsive to public desires. For the reasons outlined above, writers of this school believe that this struggle will end in failure.

Pluralism and Competition as Correctives

These arguments cannot be easily dismissed. Examples of mass irrationality, apathy, and incompetent political leadership are easily found. But the core of the argument is that accountability is impossible. Does the argument presented above prove the impossibility of obtaining accountability in government? The answer is no, but only as long as a society possesses numerous power centers and competing leadership groups. When there are numerous differing leadership groups and political institutions which permit and encourage them to compete for popular favor at the ballot box, there will be substantial popular control over government. As Pendleton Herring expressed it:

Democracy can mean government of the people, by the people, and for the people only in a symbolic sense. It is sheer poetry and to be treasured for that reason. But when democracy is analyzed, not in the language of its high prophets but in terms of its behavior, we observe that it is a system and an attitude of mind that tolerates many elites in many groups jostling and struggling.[26]

The battles between parties, the conflict of pressure groups, the competitive efforts of mass media to control public thinking and to bestow praise and blame: these are democracy's weapons against oligarchy. But Michels for one tries to dismiss even this argument by saying:

Now this ascent of new leaders always involves the danger, for those who are already in possession of power, that they will be forced to surrender their places to the new-comers. The old leader must therefore keep himself in permanent touch with the opinions and feelings of the masses to which he owes his position. Formally, at least, he must act in unison with the crowd . . . must be guided, in appearance at least, by its goodwill and pleasure. Thus it often seems as if the mass really controlled the leaders. . . . The submission of the old leaders is ostensibly an act of homage to the crowd, but *in intention* it is a means of prophylaxis against the peril by which they are threatened—the formation of a new elite.[27]

But the *intent* of the political decision-maker, when he acts in accordance with popular desires, is completely irrelevant: the *effect* under these competitive conditions is some measure of popular control over the choices of political decision-makers. Nor does this popular control occur only *after* the decision-maker acts, for political leaders in competitive politics are heavily influenced by anticipated popular reactions to their proposals.[28]

Even if the *iron law of oligarchy* is not completely satisfactory when applied to nation-states, this line of reasoning does tell us some useful things. First, democracy is impossible without competing power centers and competing leadership groups. If this competition ceases or is curtailed, the possibilities of democracy are severely limited. If potential political decision-makers are so homogeneous in background, interests, and beliefs that they refuse to compete with each other in any meaningful way, democracy also is weakened. Similarly, if the modern political division of labor and other factors result in mass apathy, modern democracy is endangered. Finally, if power corrupts impartially and universally, as Michels, Acton, and others suggest, then too the outlook for modern democracy is dim. But these things cannot be assumed, rather they are proper subjects for research. At the very least it can be said that the prophets of doom have not counted out the possibility of democracy, though they have isolated a number of possible threats to democracy. Only experience and factual analysis can tell us whether or not the oligarchical tendencies which these men see will be stronger than the institutions and the conditions which have heretofore made democracy an actuality.

Conclusions

In this chapter we have reviewed some recent empirical theories concerning the social backgrounds of political decision-makers. We have found many and substantial differences between them, but some areas of agreement seem to exist.

First, the ideas of Mosca as well as the theory of social stratification suggest that in a society with a class or caste system political decision-makers normally will be chosen from among those people of high social status. Second, writers as different in background and approach as Machiavelli, Bertrand Russell, N. S. Timasheff, and Harold Lasswell believe that political decision-makers normally will possess a political personality. Third, the same group of thinkers make the common-sense point that political decision-makers must possess certain skills and capacities in order to achieve their position, and they suggest that the skills required for adequate performance of the job are changing. For example, Lasswell sees a shift from skill at persuasion to skill in coercion. Pareto in a more elaborate theory predicted much the same development.

Virtually all the writers discussed in this chapter agree that recent social and economic changes stemming from the industrial revolution have had and will continue to have great impact on the characteristics of political decision-makers and on the way they perform their duties. Burnham sees the rise to political power of managers, Lasswell, of military men and other coercers,

Mannheim, the rise of demagogues. While their predictions differ, they are all based on the conclusion that modern conditions place a heavy strain on political democracy and the democratic way of selecting political decision-makers. They point out many threats to democracy—incompetent decision-makers, irrationality, apathy, a lack of responsiveness and accountability to popular opinion—and suggest the crucial importance of competitive access to positions of authority and the existence of a pluralistic society as antidotes to political oligarchy.

Certainly these theories are not entirely satisfactory. Nor are they all we need to know about political decision-makers. Yet in the absence of anything better, they provide the best hypothesis now available. In the following chapters we shall endeavor to see how far these generalizations are supported by the facts.

chapter three

Political Decision-Makers in the
United States

There is no shortage of facts about the lives of political decision-makers. Almost anything they do is news, and later, history. But this multitude of facts has not led to general knowledge about their social background. The historians, biographers, and journalists who have gathered most of these facts have overlooked the universal for the unique, the general for the specific. In order to obtain knowledge about the social background of political decision-makers we must be able to generalize about biography. How can this be done? What problems are raised by this approach?

How Studies of Social Background Are Made

The traditional way of obtaining insight into the lives of political decision-makers is to narrow the scope of attention to one man. With an increased understanding of his life comes a growing conviction of his special and unique characteristics.[1] But while it is certainly true that no two individuals are exactly alike, this does not mean that there are not common elements and aspects to different careers. While, for example, no two British prime ministers have been alike in all respects, they may have been similar in many ways. What is needed to obtain a new understanding of political decision-makers is an approach that emphasizes the similarities rather than the differences between them. This can be obtained only by studying groups of men.

Groups and Individuals: The General and the Particular

Students of the social background of political decision-makers may, like Charles Merriam in his *Four American Party Leaders*, or J. T. Salter in his *Boss Rule: Portraits in City Politics*, or Harold Lasswell in his *Psychopathology and Politics*, concentrate their attention upon a small number of subjects.[2] Merriam's book is based upon a study of the careers of Lincoln, Theodore Roosevelt, Wilson, and Bryan; Salter's is based on prolonged interviews with six ward politicians in Philadelphia; and Lasswell's stimulating book is based upon a relatively small number of psychological case histories. At the opposite extreme are the studies of state legislators, of members of the House of Commons, or the Hoover Institute studies of cabinet members which are based on the analysis of the backgrounds and careers of hundreds of men. Both types of studies have advantages and disadvantages.

Obviously it is risky to generalize on the basis of a relatively few cases. Studies like those of Merriam, Salter, and Lasswell do not prove anything definitively. But studies of small groups of political decision-makers do permit a thorough attention to detail that is inevitably denied to analysts concerned with larger groups. Furthermore it is easier "to rise above the data" and to formulate fruitful hypotheses when not confronted with a glut of facts to be processed. As Professor Oliver Garceau recently put it:

. . . so long as new insights, new variables and new relationships can be seen through unsystematic examination . . . it would be a mistake to restrict political behavior research to system, rigor and quantification, in the false illusion that this alone is science.[3]

Until social background research no longer requires the elaboration of hypotheses but only their verification, exploratory studies of small groups will have an important contribution to make.

Studies of political decision-makers in large aggregates likewise have advantages and disadvantages. A researcher can never conduct as detailed an investigation of a large number of men as he can of a few. A study of a large group must almost inevitably be abstract and quantitative in nature, must concentrate so heavily upon the average and the typical that it may overlook the existence of the splendid and significant exceptions. Despite these dangers, the quantitative study of large aggregates of people can provide a degree of positive results which the more qualitative studies cannot. When hypotheses can be expressed in such a way as to be quantitatively tested, this type of research is highly desirable and useful.

Thus the strengths of the quantifiers and qualifiers complement each other: one approach is weak where the other is strong. Both types of research can contribute to greater political knowledge. It is the attempt to generalize about the lives of political decision-makers and not the number of persons studied which differentiates the modern approach from traditional biography.

Sources of Data

Ideally the student of groups of political decision-makers should go about his work in the same fashion as a biographer. Interviews with his subjects, analysis of their private files and correspondence, discussions with their friends, enemies, and colleagues are all indispensable ways of learning in detail about their lives and backgrounds. These sources can be used by the student of relatively small groups. But if the subject of the study is a rather large number of men, the extensive use of these research techniques is, for practical reasons, impossible. Even the most indefatigable worker cannot be expected to complete several hundred detailed biographies in a lifetime. Thus most students of the social backgrounds of large groups have relied primarily upon other sources, less satisfactory but also less onerous, for most of their facts.

One popular device used by researchers in this field is the mail questionnaire.[4] After some preliminary analysis and planning, the researcher decides exactly what he would like to know about his subjects, devises a form that elicits this information and mails it to the subjects of his study. The advantage of this procedure is obvious: it is thus possible to approach a large number of people quickly and inexpensively. The drawbacks, however, are severe. It is virtually impossible to obtain a complete return, and those who do return the filled-out questionnaire are seldom a representative sample of the entire group. The questionnaire itself must be brief and self-explanatory or else returns will be greatly diminished and the answers confusing. Finally this approach can only be used if one is studying contemporary political decision-makers. Thus while the mail questionnaire is often a useful and convenient way of collecting biographical facts about a large number of people, its limitations usually require that it be used in conjunction with other devices.

Even more popular sources of information are biographical directories. These range from such as the *Dictionary of National Biography* and the *Dictionary of American Biography*, which contain rather long articles, to the multitude of *Who's Who* volumes with their short sketches reproduced in microscopic print.[5] Although biographical directories are indispensable to researchers in this field, they can also be exasperating to use. The researcher quickly finds that the volumes with long articles are severely selective in their coverage. Thus, for example, a student of American Congressmen in the nineteenth century would discover that many if not most of his subjects are not included in these volumes. Many of those who are included will have been the subjects of more adequate book-length works. On the other hand, the directories with shorter articles on each man are more inclusive in their coverage but contain only a minimum of information. Moreover the data included in these sketches is controlled by their subjects. This means that the researcher obtains only those facts that the subject wishes to make public, and different directories intended for different audiences will often contain quite different pictures of the man. The only way to avoid such distortions is to consult as many published biographical sources as possible for each man.

A final source of information about the lives of political decision-makers is popular biography. The daily, weekly, and monthly press both in the United States and abroad contains a tremendous amount of biographical information. It is usually slanted but, when cautiously used, is an excellent source of facts. Some popular biography is indexed[6] and thus readily available to the researcher. Most of it is not. The material that is not indexed is most accessible in newspaper morgues or obituary columns.

Obviously there are many sources of information about the social background of political decision-makers, yet no source is entirely adequate. Those engaged in research in this field must reconcile themselves to the use of a number of different sources which sometimes yield conflicting facts and conclusions.

After these general remarks about the ways in which studies of social background are made, we are in a position to look at some of their results. In the following pages we shall discuss those findings of empirical studies of political decision-makers in the United States, Great Britain, Germany, and the Soviet Union which are relevant to the theoretical questions raised in Chapter Two. For the United States we shall be concerned with only three of the questions suggested by the theorists. What is the impact of social class upon the recruitment of political decision-makers? What are their usual skills and personality characteristics? What are the effects of these characteristics on the conduct of government? In the cases of Great Britain, Germany, and the Soviet Union we shall be concerned with a single question: what is the relationship between the social characteristics of political decision-makers and social and political change? Unfortunately the limitations of space and of the coverage of available studies make impossible a discussion of all four questions for each country.

Social Class and Political Recruitment

The mythology of American politics is heavily influenced by a log-cabin to White House motif. Despite the growing evidence of class distinctions in American society,[7] the notion persists that politics is one area of life in which the American dream can come true. The theories analyzed in Chapter Two, however, suggest that this view is unrealistic. Regardless of democratic institutions and values, political decision-makers will tend to be chosen from among those ranking high in America's system of social stratification. Which view is correct? When the scattered studies of American political personnel are drawn together, they supply us with a reasonably trustworthy answer to this question.

Father's Occupation

Probably the most important single criterion for social ranking in the United States is occupation. Although it is by no means a certain index to an individual's social standing in the community, occupation is perhaps the closest approach to an infallible guide. Thus information on the occupations of the fathers of American political decision-makers provides a reasonably accurate picture of their class origins. As is plainly evident in Table 1, those American political decision-makers *for whom this information is available* are, with very few exceptions, sons of professional men, proprietors and officials, and farmers. A very small minority were sons of wage earners, low-salaried workers, farm laborers or servants. When this fact is compared with the occupational distribution of the labor force in 1890 (about the median time of birth of all

TABLE 1

Occupational Class of Fathers of American Political Decision-Makers
(In Percentages)

Occupational Class of Father	President, Vice-president, Cabinet 1789–1934	High Level Civil Servant 1940	U.S. Senators 81st Congress 1949–51	U.S. Representatives** 77th Congress 1941–43	Labor Force 1890
Professional	38	28	22	31	5
Proprietors & officials	20	30	33	31	6
Farmers	38	29	40	29	26
Low salaried workers	*	3	1	0	5
Wage earners	4	10	3	9	36
Servants	0	0	0	0	7
Farm laborers	0	0	0	0	15
Unknown, unclassified	0	0	1	0	0
	100 (n=311)	100 (n=180)	100 (n=109)	100 (n=186)	100

* Less than 1.
** Subject to substantial error because of incomplete data.

these groups except the first), the narrow base from which political decision-makers appear to be recruited is clear.

If this were all the evidence available, conclusions about the relationship between social stratification and political life chances would have to be extremely tentative. Fortunately a great deal of other relevant data exists.

Race

Perhaps the most striking feature of the American system of stratification is the castelike position of the Negro. If there is a tendency for those with low social positions to be denied important political office in the United States, then one would expect few if any Negroes to become political decision-makers, despite the fact that they constitute approximately ten per cent of the population. This seems to have been the case. About the only important federal offices held by Negroes have been in Congress. As can be seen in Table 2,

TABLE 2

Negroes in Congress: 1869–1950

Congress	Number in House	Number in Senate
41st	2	1
42nd	5	0
43rd	7	0
44th	7	1
45th	3	1
46th	0	1
47th	1	0
48th	2	0
49th	2	0
50th	0	0
51st	3	0
52nd	1	0
53rd	1	0
54th	1	0
55th	1	0
56th	1	0
57th to 71st	0	0
72nd	1	0
73rd	1	0
74th	1	0
75th	1	0
76th	1	0
77th	1	0
78th	1	0
79th	2	0
80th	2	0
81st	2	0

Negroes were elected to the House and appointed to the Senate in small numbers from the southern states during the Reconstruction Period. As white supremacy was gradually re-established in the South, the number of Negroes in Congress declined until they disappeared entirely from Capitol Hill about 1900 and did not again win seats in the Congress until the Negroes became politically powerful in some northern, urban congressional districts during the

New Deal. Since the Negroes are gradually bettering their economic and social position, one should expect them to be more numerous among political decision-makers in the future. To date, however, their political opportunities have been extremely poor.

Ethnic Origins

The situation with regard to members of nationality groups in the United States is far less clear. Denied access to many other areas of endeavor, immigrants and the sons of immigrants seem to have become unusually active in American politics. In many areas of the country it is a positive political advantage to be a first- or second-generation American as long as one is a member of the dominant ethnic group. Thus in the 1950 Mayoralty election in New York all three major candidates were born in Italy. Harold Zink in his study of *City Bosses in the United States*[8] found that three quarters of the bosses were either foreign-born or second-generation Americans and that they usually were members of one of the largest ethnic groups in their respective cities.

But if the fragmentary evidence at our command is to be trusted, as the public offices become more important, fewer first- and second-generation Americans are chosen as political decision-makers. As can be seen in Table 3, the proportion of United States Senators who were foreign-born has fluctuated considerably since 1789. Beginning at the rather high figure of 15%, it has declined to a mere 2% at present, while always paralleling the rise and fall in the numbers of the foreign-born in the population at large. But regardless of

TABLE 3

Percentage of Senators and of Total Population Who Were Foreign-Born
(Selected Dates, 1789–1949)

	1789	1845	1895–1905	1913	1923	1933	1941	1945	1949–1951
Senators	15	2	8	5	3	4	3	4	2
Population*	——	11	14	15	13	12	9	8	7**

* Nearest census.
** White only.

the times there consistently has been a smaller proportion of immigrants among Senators than among the population as a whole.

Not only when a person or his ancestors came to the United States but also his national origin are relevant factors in determining his over-all social status. Again information is scanty, being available and reliable only for the members of the 81st Congress. As can be seen from Table 4, almost all of the first- and second-generation Congressmen and Senators were drawn from the old immigration groups from northwestern and central Europe and Canada, only a small proportion from eastern and southern Europe and Asia.

Thus our very limited factual evidence suggests that although foreign birth or ancestry are not absolute barriers to important public offices, they are likely to be handicaps for those aspiring to more than local prominence. As nationality groups come of age[9] politically in certain localities an occasional member becomes a decision-maker. Except in such instances membership in minority nationality groups seems to be a political disadvantage at the present time.

TABLE 4

Origins of Foreign-Born and Second-Generation Senators
and Representatives, 81st Congress (1949–1951)
(In Percentages)

Region*	Foreign-Born			Second-Generation		
	Senators	Repre-sentatives	Popula-tion (1940)	Senators	Repre-sentatives	Popula-tion (1940)
Northwestern Europe	0	50	23	75	53	29
Central Europe	50	33	31	19	30	34
Eastern Europe	0	0	13	0	1	9
Southern Europe	0	0	17	6	10	14
Other Europe	0	0	**	0	0	1
Asia	0	0	1	0	1	1
America	50	17	13	0	5	11
All other	0	0	1	0	0	1
	100 (n=2)	100 (n=6)	99	100 (n=16)	100 (n=88)	100

* Northwestern Europe includes the British Isles, Scandinavia except Finland, the Low Countries, France, and Switzerland. Central Europe includes Germany, Poland, Czechoslovakia, Austria, Hungary, Yugoslavia. Eastern Europe includes the USSR, Baltic States, Finland, Rumania, Bulgaria, and European Turkey. Southern Europe includes Greece, Italy, Spain, Portugal; Asia includes Palestine, Syria, Asian Turkey, and other Asiatic countries; America includes all the American continent less the West Indies; All other includes Australia, etc.
** Less than .5%

Religion

Given the previous data, it is not surprising that evidence, again incomplete, suggests that an American's chance of becoming a decision-maker is heavily influenced by his religion. By studying Table 5 the reader can see that Protestant denominations with congregations of high social status (Congregational, Presbyterian, Episcopal, Unitarian) possess about twice the number of Representatives and Senators they would have if Congressmen were completely representative in their religions. The Methodists, Lutherans and Baptists have about the right number. On the other hand, Roman Catholics have only one-half to one-third and Jews, one-third to one-sixth the number of Congressmen they should have if the Congress is to be a religious cross-section of the nation. As far as the Senate and House are concerned, then, a Protestant has better than average opportunities while Catholics and Jews have more limited ones.

But the effect of religious affiliation on political chances does not depend alone upon the prestige of the sect. Whether a man of a given religion stands a chance of becoming a political decision-maker or not also depends upon what religion is dominant in the section of the country in which he lives. There appears to be a tendency for voters to cast their ballots for persons having a religious affiliation similar to their own.[10] But despite this tendency, Congress is far from an accurate reflection of the religious composition of the American people, and the distortion is in favor of the religious views of the upper and upper-middle classes.

TABLE 5

Religious Affiliation of United States Senators and Representatives 77th, 78th, 81st Congresses
(In Percentages)

Religion	77th Congress Senate	77th Congress House	78th Congress Senate	78th Congress House	81st Congress Senate	81st Congress House	Total Claimed Membership (1950)
Protestant	81	70	85	74	87	83	59
Congregational	7	3	6	4	6	4	6
Presbyterian	11	13	17	12	12	12	4
Episcopal	10	11	17	10	10	12	3
Unitarian	1 } 29	1 } 28	2 } 42	1 } 27	1 } 29	1 } 29	* } 13
Methodist	22	17	18	17	17	22	13
Lutheran	2	4	2	3	4	4	7
Baptist	10 } 34	11 } 32	12 } 32	12 } 32	13 } 34	12 } 38	20 } 40
Disciples of Christ	2	3	3	3	2	0	2
Mormon	2	0	2	1	3	0	1
Society of Friends	1	0	2	0	2	1	*
Church of Christ, Scientist	1	0	1	1	1	0	**
Christian Church	0	0	0	2	4	4	**
Unspecified and other	12	6	3	8	11	12	3
Roman Catholic	11	20	10	18	12	16	34
Jewish	0	2	0	2	1	1	6
Other	0	0	3	0	0	0	1
None	4	1	2	0	0	0	0
Unknown	3	6		6	0	0	0
	99	99	100	100	100	100	100
	(n=96)	(n=435)	(n=96)	(n=435)	(n=109)	(n=289)	

* Less than .5%
** Membership figures may not be published.

27

Education

It would be a mistake if the reader assumed from what has been said so far that American political decision-makers are chosen solely upon the basis of fortunate birth or cultural inheritance. Such a head start helps, yet it alone is not enough. Americans must also display a considerable amount of personal achievement before their political chances are very good. Perhaps the best indication of this is the fact that political decision-makers are among the most educated of all occupational groups in the United States. (See Table 6.) There is a good deal of variation in educational level within the group, but it is true that a vast majority of them have been selected in recent years from the 10% or so of the adult population who have attended college. Moreover although the long-range trend has been toward more highly educated decision-makers, they appear always to have been greatly superior in education to the citizens at large.[11]

This high level of educational achievement among the American political decision-makers is extremely desirable. But while the American educational system is one of the most equalitarian in the world, substantial differences in educational opportunities do exist between social classes. Financial pressure, lack of motivation for academic success, the unconscious preference of middle-class teachers for middle-class children, and so on, place the child from a working-class family at a distinct disadvantage to his middle- or upper-class counterpart even when their intelligence is the same.[12] Therefore without alterations in the present American educational system, the higher the informal educational requirements are set for political decision-makers, the more unequal become the political life chances of Americans.

Occupation

All of the facts presented so far in this section suggest that the log cabin to White House myth is rather far from the truth. For the most part political decision-makers are far from common men in either their origins or their achievements. This conclusion is greatly strengthened by the facts about their occupational backgrounds.

The results of a number of efforts to determine the occupational levels* of recent political decision-makers are presented in Table 7. According to these studies, about 90% of each group in the table are drawn from the top 15% or so of the labor force. However as the importance of the public office declines, we find a gradual decline in the occupational status of its usual incumbent. Thus, for example, the state legislatures appear to be far more "democratic" in composition than the Congress of the United States or the state governorships. Moreover while empirical studies of historical trends in the occupational distribution of political decision-makers are scarce, the evidence that does exist suggests that their occupational level has not changed a great deal during the last century and a half.[13]

---

* Many political decision-makers have spent virtually all their adult lives in public affairs. Others have had many different occupations; a smaller number have pursued several occupations at one time. Under such circumstances classification is difficult and can easily become arbitrary. Despite these difficulties, conscientious efforts to determine the principal nonpolitical occupations of decision-makers can reduce the number of difficult cases to a few and thus give a reasonably accurate picture.

Table 6

Educational Level of American Political Decision-Makers
(In Percentages)

Highest Level Attained	Presidents, Vice-presidents, Cabinet members (1877–1934)	Supreme Court Justices (1897–1937)	United States Senators (1949–51)	United States Representatives (1941–43)	High-level Civil Servants (1940)	State Governors (1930–40)	Missouri State Legislators (1901–31)	Population over 25 years of age (1940)
None	0	0	0	0	0	0	0	5
Grade school	11	0	3	0	0	3	30	54
High school	10	0	10	12	7	20	13	31
College	79	100	87	88	93	77	57	10
	100	100	100	100	100	100	100	100
	(n=176)	(n=20)	(n=108)	(n=431)	(n=242)	(n=135)	(n=2,876)	

29

TABLE 7

Occupational Class of American Political Decision-Makers
(In Percentages)

Occupational Class	President, Vice-president, Cabinet* 1877–1934	United States Senators 1949–51	United States Representatives 1949–51	State Governors 1930–40	State Legislators** 1925–35	Labor Force 1940
Professionals	74	69	69	60	36	7
Lawyers	70 }	57 }	56 }	52 }	28 }	
Others	4 }	12 }	13 }	8 }	8 }	
Proprietors & officials	21	24	22	25	25	8
Farmers	2	7	4	11	22	11
Low-salaried workers	1	0	1	1	4	17
Wage earners	2	0	2	1	3	40
Servants	0	0	0	0	0	11
Farm laborers	0	0	0	0	0	7
Unknown, unclassified	0	0	2	3	10	0
	100 (n=176)	100 (n=109)	100 (n=435)	101 (n=170)	100 (n=12,689)	101

* Occupations in this column are those for which presidents, vice-presidents, and cabinet officers were trained.

** Figures for the lower houses of 13 selected states and the upper houses of 12. The states are Arkansas, California (lower house only), Illinois, Indiana, Iowa, Louisiana, Maine, Minnesota, Mississippi, New Jersey, New York, Pennsylvania, Washington.

Lawyers: High Priests of American Politics

One small occupational group, the legal profession, has supplied a large majority of America's top-level public officials throughout our entire history. Twenty-five of the 52 signers of the Declaration of Independence were lawyers, 31 of the 55 members of the Continental Congress, 23 out of the 33 men who have served as President of the United States have been lawyers.[14] Another look at Table 7 will indicate that the legal profession, comprising about one-tenth of one per cent of the labor force, still supplies a majority of American decision-makers. Why this predominance of lawyers?

Lawyers meet what seems to be the first prerequisite of top-level political leadership: they are in a high-prestige occupation. But so are physicians, businessmen, and scientists. Why are lawyers dominant in politics rather than members of these other high-prestige groups? Certainly any attempt to explain the origins and development of American political leaders must be able to account for this.

The answer to these questions can be found in the skills of the lawyer and the nature of the legal profession in America. The skills developed by the lawyer in the practice of his profession give him an advantage in the race for office, if not actual training for the performance of public duties. His job involves skill in interpersonal mediation and conciliation and facility in the use of words. Both of these skills are indispensable to the politician. Moreover the

lawyer in private practice operates in large part as the expert adviser to decision-makers. As Lasswell and McDougal put it:

. . . the lawyer is to-day . . . the one indispensable adviser of every responsible
policy-maker of our society—whether we speak of the head of a government department or agency, of the executive of a corporation or labor union, of the secre-
tary of a trade or other private association, or even of the humble independent
enterpriser or professional man. As such an adviser the lawyer, when informing
his policy-maker of what he can or cannot legally do, is in an unassailably strategic
position to influence, if not create, policy . . . For better or worse our decision-
makers and our lawyers are bound together in a relation of dependence or of identity.[15]

With the development of these skills in the normal course of an occupational
career, the lawyer is at a substantial advantage over the average layman who
decides to enter politics.

The position of the legal profession in American society must be considered
as another factor contributing to the lawyers' political dominance. Unlike
many other countries the United States has never had a landed aristocracy
with a tradition of public service. While most political decision-makers enjoy
high-prestige positions, few are the possessors of inherited wealth. In a highly
competitive society in which occupational success is the most highly valued
goal for the ambitious, who can with the least danger leave their jobs for the
tremendous risks of a political career? Among the high-prestige occupations
the answer seems to be the lawyers. Certainly other professionals find the
neglect of their careers for political activities extremely hazardous. In the pro-
fessions in which the subject matter is changing rapidly, such as medicine,
science, and engineering, with a few years of neglect special skills are either
lost or become outmoded.[16] The active businessman, either an individual
entrepreneur or a member of a corporate bureaucracy, usually finds neglect of
his vocation for politics no asset to his primary occupational interest. Politics is
demanding more and more time from its practitioners. A man who actively
manages a farm finds it difficult to indulge a taste for politics under these
conditions.

These barriers to sustained political activity either do not exist or are de-
creased in significance for the lawyer. For the most part the law changes relatively slowly, and a lawyer-politician is usually in a position to keep up with
such changes while active in politics. The lawyer who typically is in solo practice or a member of a small law firm is dispensable.[17] He can easily combine
his occupation on a part-time basis with political activity. This activity may be
an actual advantage to his occupational advancement. Free and professionally
legitimate advertising, contacts, and opportunities to meet other (often important) lawyers of his area result from his political activities, to say nothing
of possible appointments to judicial office. Thus a lawyer entering political
life does not cut himself off from the possibilities of occupational success; indeed he may actually enhance such prospects. This is not the case for other
high-prestige occupations.

Thus the facts about the occupational backgrounds of American political
decision-makers indicate that more than high social status is necessary in order
to have high political opportunities. Some positions of high social status may
actually be a detriment to the politically ambitious. But where high prestige is

32   *The Social Background*

combined with training in interpersonal relations, easy access to politics, and "dispensability," as is the case for the lawyers, the result is a dominant position in American politics.

Is There a Ruling Class in the United States?

After this brief review of some of the findings of empirical studies of American political decision-makers, we are in a position to answer the question with which we began: is there a ruling class in the United States?

Certainly not as the elite and ruling-class theorists use the term! We have found that the public officials who make the most important political decisions in the United States are a fairly heterogeneous lot. There are substantial differences in their origins and experiences. It is also evident that the avenues to positions of political power are not completely closed even to relatively low-status groups such as Negroes, immigrants, and the poorly educated. But this same evidence shows that political opportunities tend to be best for those in positions near the top of the American class system and worst for those near the bottom. As a result our political decision-makers, taken as a whole, are very far from being a cross section of the electorate. Rather there seems to be a sort of class ranking of public offices in the United States—the more important the office, the higher the social status of its normal incumbent. Thus incumbents in the top offices are mostly upper- and upper-middle-class people.

It would be a mistake to attribute this fact to any kind of conscious plot. Such a point of view is hardly justified. What seems to happen in the United States is far simpler than this. First, there is the obvious fact that the money[18] and time necessary for sustained political activity are possessed by only a minority of the American people. The higher up the social scale an individual is, the more likely he is to possess these prerequisites, although even some high-prestige groups do not have both. Second, opportunities to obtain the requisite status, time, and money are far from equal. Studies of stratification in America show with monotonous regularity that a head start helps in the race for social success. The same is true of one's chances for obtaining advanced education and professional skills. Finally it seems understandable in a society with an accepted stratification system for the electorate to choose men with high social status to represent them in the decision-making process. A man with a fairly high social position has met the society's definition of success. Rightly or wrongly the lawyer is thought to be a better man than the factory worker. Thus when the factory worker votes for the lawyer he is voting for a man who is what he would *like* to be. All of these factors and perhaps even more are involved in explaining the impact of social class on the nature of America's top-level political personnel.

Another warning is in order. It is misleading to assume that a group must literally be represented among the political decision-makers to have influence or political power. The unrepresentative nature of America's political decision-makers no doubt has its consequences, but it does not free them from their ultimate accountability to the electorate at large. Thus the frequency with which members of certain groups are found among decision-makers should not be considered an infallible index of the distribution of power in a society. In America at least lower-status groups have political power far in excess of their number in Congress, the Cabinet, and so on. And there seems to be some evidence that those at the very apex of the social hierarchy are also represented not literally but by sympathetic agents such as lawyers and professional politicians.[19]

Factors Other Than Socioeconomic Status

Perhaps the best way to place in proper perspective the impact of the class structure upon the recruitment of American political personnel is to note that other social factors unrelated to class have a substantial effect as well. For instance, one of the most striking characteristics of American political decision-makers is their advanced age. Presidents are most often elected to office when they are from 55 to 59 years of age, and a vast majority of Supreme Court Justices, Senators, Representatives, and top-level civil servants are over 50.[20] Until recently women were unknown among the decision-makers, and more than thirty years after the granting of federal suffrage very few can be found in high public office.[21] Taken together, this age and sex discrimination limits the number of Americans with good chances of becoming decision-makers as much as or even more than does class discrimination. Similarly it seems that high public officials originate in unusually large numbers in rural areas and small towns, and that those with early urban environments suffer from a political disadvantage. On the other hand, disproportionately large numbers of political decision-makers reside in urban areas and are as a group more geographically mobile than the average American.[22] Thus political opportunities are affected quite substantially by factors other than class. And of course an individual who becomes a political decision-maker must have the desire, luck, skill, and endurance necessary to exploit his opportunities. The class structure is only one important factor influencing who achieves power. An exclusively class explanation of leadership recruitment in the United States would be as misleading as one which totally ignored its importance.

Personality and Skills

Many students of politics believe that political decision-makers are characterized by the possession of special personalities and skills, that an individual becomes a political decision-maker at least in part because of certain personal qualities or traits (see Chapter Two). Similar views are held by many psychologists interested in leadership. As a result a large number of empirical studies, ranging from the most impressionistic to the most rigorously experimental, have been made of the personal qualities or traits of various kinds of leaders.

Leadership Traits

These empirical studies suggest a large number of traits of the leader. F. H. Allport, for instance, developed the following list in 1924:[23]

Ascendance	Expansiveness
Physical strength	High intelligence
High motility	Understanding
Tonus	Susceptibility to social stimulation
Erect, aggressive carriage	Tact
Tenacity	Zeal
Face-to-face mode of address	Social participation
Energy	Character
Restraint	Drive
Inscrutability	

More recently E. S. Bogardus has reduced the number of leadership traits to five:[24]

Imagination	Versatility
Foresight	Inhibition
Flexibility	

After a painstaking analysis of more than one hundred recent books and articles on leadership, Stogdill concludes that the characteristics most often associated with leadership are:[25]

Capacity (including intelligence, alertness, verbal facility, original-
ity, judgment)

Achievement (including scholarship, knowledge, athletic accomplishments)

Responsibility (including dependability, initiative, persistence, ag-
gressiveness, self confidence, desire to excel)

Participation (activity, sociability, cooperation, adaptability, humor)

Status (socio-economic position, popularity)

Despite some agreement among the many studies in this field, their most striking characteristic is the amount of disagreement found among them. According to Stogdill, recent studies have found that leaders were both younger and older, taller and shorter, heavier and lighter, more extroverted and more introverted, more and less emotionally stable than their followers. Similarly some studies show that leaders have better health, appearance, intel-ligence, and academic records than their followers, and still other studies indi-cate that these factors are unrelated to leadership.

The contradictory findings of studies of leadership traits are in all likelihood the result of the confused conception of leadership held by many researchers in this field. For the most part studies of leadership traits have been based on the (often unexpressed) assumption that the same skills and traits are required to be a leader in all situations and circumstances. Thus the leaders in kindergarten play, adolescent gangs, college-campus activities, and national politics were expected to possess the same traits. The contradictory answers obtained when studying leaders in these different situations plus the gradual recognition that being a leader in one area of life may place quite different demands on the individual from the demands of leadership in another have led to an almost complete abandonment of this position in recent years. "There is no one leadership type of personality,"[26] writes one student, and another spells out his objections to past reasearch in these words:

A person does not become a leader by virtue of the possession of some combination of traits, but the pattern of personal characteristics of the leader must bear
some relevant relationship to the characteristics, activities, and goals of the
followers.[27]

In other words recent research suggests that the assumption of universal lead-ership traits is false and that politically successful persons will in all likelihood possess different personalities and skills from those of business leaders, student leaders, and other types of leaders. Therefore the only way to discover the traits and skills of decision-makers is to study men who are practicing poli-ticians.

Traits and Skills of American Politicians

Compared to the number of studies attempting to catalog universal traits of leadership, those specifically concerned with American political leaders are exceedingly scarce. Prepared by political scientists, they are not as methodologically rigorous as the studies previously discussed. And since politicians are extremely busy and often important men, it is next to impossible to obtain detailed information about their personalities based upon psychological testing under controlled conditions. Nevertheless several attempts have been made to determine the traits of the politician in America.

Charles Merriam,[28] for example, near the end of a lifetime of observation of politics, concluded that the successful politician usually possesses a number of specific personal traits or skills. First, successful politicians have a *high degree of social sensitivity*, an ability quickly and accurately to sense changes in the public mood and the distribution of power. Second, they possess a *high degree of facility in personal contacts* with a wide range of people of varying backgrounds and opinions. Third, they have *ability to make and handle group contacts*. They must be able "to know and reckon with" conflicting group demands. Fourth, the modern politician possesses *ability in dramatic expression and facility in invention* of "formulas, policies and ideologies" to meet changing circumstance. Finally, the politician possesses a high degree of *courage*.

Other students of politics have suggested alternative lists of traits and skills. J. T. Salter, for example, suggests eleven general characteristics of the American politician:

. . . (1) they stick everlastingly at it; (2) they know that the Kingdom of Heaven is taken by violence; (3) they live decades among their people and learn to judge their wants; (4) have a flair for getting along with people; (5) have problem-solving ability; (6) understand that politics is a science of the possible; (7) are able to dramatize their appeal so as to effectively capture favorable attention; (8) often have an unusual memory for names and people; (9) can gauge public sentiment and strength of various group attitudes; (10) have the kind of courage that enables the possessor to risk all on the outcome of an election and then be able to start building anew in case of defeat; and (11) have enough vision and imagination to see over the district for which they are candidates, whether this be a township or all forty-eight states.[29]

These and similar efforts to determine the traits and skills of American politicians are interesting but impressionistic and unreliable. Unfortunately more systematic studies are almost nonexistent.[30]

The lack of reliability of this approach, however, is not its greatest weakness, for even a reliable list of traits without any indication of their relative importance or interrelations would be of limited usefulness to political analysis. Moreover some of the traits found in the various studies seem to overlap, while others seem to conflict. Often no attempt is made to distinguish between traits facilitating the achievement of leadership position and its retention. But the principal weakness of this type of research is that it is based on a misleading conception of human personality. Personality is not the sum of the traits of which it is made. To assume this is

. . . to ignore one of the fundamental properties of personality, its possession of *organization*. The same 'trait' will function differently in personalities which are organized differently . . . It is only when attention is paid to arrangement or position that organization, as such, can be brought into account.[31]

The trait approach completely ignores this important fact.

These studies are not completely useless, however, because they contain some useful data for the student of political decision-makers. But the possibility of a greater understanding of these individuals in the future depends primarily upon the exploration of their personality structure rather than upon the cataloging of discrete and isolated traits.

Types of Political Personalities

By far the most fruitful work on the personality of political decision-makers has been done by Harold Lasswell.[32] As we saw in Chapter Two, Lasswell has come to believe, after analyzing a number of life histories, that the principal motivation for political activity is emotional insecurity and a low esteem of the self, developed early in life. This psychological condition and the compensatory drive for power may be the result of many factors: an early life in which parental affection and indulgence are contingent upon success and in which failure is met by harsh discipline and deprivation, or one in which the parents project their frustrated ambitions upon their children; membership in a marginal group within the society; thwarted expectations for the future; and the possession of physical defects or the experience of severe illness. All these may result in a shriveled ego and an extreme demand for deference. Such a condition, however, does not always result in a compensatory search for power. In many cases it may result in total withdrawal from politics and an increase in striving for success in other areas of life. But under certain conditions—when the individual also possesses both the opportunities and skills necessary for a political career—men and women suffering from a low esteem of the self will attempt to compensate for it by seeking political power.

In his exploration of the mental and emotional lives of power seekers, Lasswell has found that their personalities fall into two "ideal types"—agitators and administrators.*

The essential mark of the agitator is the high value which he places upon the emotional response of the public. Whether he attacks or defends social institutions is a secondary matter. The agitator has come by his name honestly, for he is enough agitated about public policy to communicate his excitement to those about him. He idealizes the magnitude of the desirable social changes which are capable of being produced by a specific line of social action . . . The agitator easily infers that he who disagrees with him is in communion with the devil, and that opponents show bad faith or timidity. Agitators are notoriously contentious and undisciplined . . . The agitator is willing to subordinate personal considerations to the superior claims of principle. Children may suffer while father and mother battle for the "cause" . . . Ever on the alert for pernicious intrusions of private interest into public affairs, the agitator sees "unworthy" motives where others see the just claims of friendship. Believing in direct, emotional responses from the public, the agitator trusts in mass appeals and general principles. Many of his kind live to shout and write . . . They become frustrated and confused in the tangled mass of technical detail upon which successful administration depends.[33]

---

* A word of warning is in order about Lasswell's two types of political personalities. Lasswell does not intend to imply that all elected officials are agitators and all bureaucrats are administrative types.

This kind of behavior is the result of a number of factors.

Agitators as a class are strongly narcissistic types. Narcissism is encouraged by obstacles in the early love relationships, or by overindulgence and admiration in the family circle. Libido which is blocked in moving outward toward objects settles back on the self . . . and a strong homosexual component is thus characteristic. Among the agitators this yearning for emotional response of the homosexual kind is displaced upon generalized objects, and high value is placed upon arousing emotional responses from the community at large. The tremendous urge for expression in written or spoken language is a roundabout method of gratifying these underlying emotional drives . . . The family history shows much repression of the direct manifestation of hatred.[34]

The administrative type of political personality, on the other hand, is characterized not by dramatic but by compulsive behavior.

The compulsive character will select less varied objects for displacement and rationalization than the [agitator] dramatizer. The impulsive inclines toward carefully defined limits and the well-worked-out ordering of parts; the dramatizer excels in scope and abundance of loosely classified detail. The hallmark of the former is the imposition of uniformity, while the latter tolerates diversity and excels in nuance. The compulsive desubjectivizes a situation, while the dramatizer remains sensitive to psychological dimensions; the one denies novelty, while the other welcomes it; one squeezes and compresses the dimensions of the human situation which the other complies with and allows to spread. The compulsive monotonizes the presentation of the self to the other, while the latter multiplies the faces and façades which can be presented to other persons.[35]

The principal difference according to Lasswell between the life histories of the administrators and those of the agitators is that the administrators are unable for a number of possible reasons to displace their feelings upon remote and abstract objects as are the agitators.

Lasswell's ideas are by no means pure speculation. His theorizing has far outrun the available empirical data, but a fair amount of case-history material exists which seems generally in accord with his ideas.[36] Yet much of this material comes from the clinical records of the mentally ill. This certainly may introduce distortion and exaggeration into his findings. It is very true that much can be learned about normal personality from the study of the abnormal, but it is also true that differences in degree can become large enough to become differences in kind. Some may feel that this is true of Lasswell's analysis of the personalities of politicians, that it is valid only for sick politicians and not for all politicians. Although the limited amount of evidence available on the personality structures of normal power seekers suggests that this is not the case, it may be possible after more detailed research on normal politicians to develop a more elaborate typology (with fewer mixed types than the present agitator-administrative, dramatic-compulsive dichotomies) than that now used by Lasswell. Then it may appear that the political personality is less pathological than the Lasswell analysis seems to imply.

Summary

The study of the personalities of political decision-makers is still in its infancy, but real progress is being made. The early research on leadership traits was either systematic and rigorous but largely irrelevant to the political scientists, or else highly relevant but also impressionistic and unreliable. With the introduction of the new emphasis on personality structure, the research in this field escaped from the horns of this dilemma. Practical problems of doing research in this area are still immense, requiring special training and access to very detailed case-history material, and theoretical problems still abound, but it is safe to say that this is one of the most challenging and fruitful areas of modern political research.

Effects on the Conduct of Government

The ultimate aim of research on the social backgrounds of political decision-makers is to contribute to a better understanding of their behavior and thus to a clearer view of the entire governmental process (see Chapter One). Attempts to determine the relationship between social backgrounds and the conduct of government thus constitute the really critical stage in this sort of research. Unfortunately very little empirical work has been focused on this task to date; and that which has been so directed has not been completely satisfactory.

Beard: An Economic Interpretation of the Constitution

The first and probably the most famous attempt to show the impact of the social backgrounds of political decision-makers on the conduct of American government was Charles Beard's *An Economic Interpretation of the Constitution* (1913).[37] In this book Beard found that the members of the Constitutional Convention of 1787 were mostly well-to-do professional men, merchants, manufacturers, and planters, and that many of them were speculators in public credit and land. Since political and economic stability was in the economic interest of these groups, Beard concludes that:

The overwhelming majority of members, at least five-sixths, were immediately, directly and personally interested in the outcome of their labor at Philadelphia, and were to a greater or less extent economic beneficiaries from the adoption of the Constitution.[38]

But does this mean that the authors of the Constitution wrote it and popularized it *because* they would gain financially from such a policy? Not necessarily. Nor do these facts necessarily imply that the Constitution was in its origins a class document. The founding fathers, no less than modern politicians, had to act within the limits of what they thought the electorate, admittedly restricted but still far more "representative" than the founding fathers themselves, would bear. And, *judged by the standards of the eighteenth century*, neither the Constitution nor the method of its ratification were especially biased by class distinctions.

The Beard study does indicate however, that the authors of the American Constitution, like all political decision-makers before and since their time, acted from a mixture of motives, some public, some private. The end product of their deliberations during the hot Philadelphia summer of 1787 was the result of many factors and not just one. Before an adequate understanding of political decision-making is possible, we must be able to determine what these factors were and assess their relative weights. The Beard analysis of the Constitutional Convention overlooks this problem by concentrating on only a single factor in the political equation.

Legislative Voting Behavior

Almost all attempts to determine the influence of social background on the behavior of American political decision-makers have been made by students of the legislative process, and for good reason: the necessary data is readily available. Both biographical information and the legislator's position on roll-call votes are published for most legislative bodies. The biographical data is sometimes inadequate and an exclusive concern for the legislator's actions in the roll-call situation overlooks a great deal, but an attempt to relate the two is certainly a beginning of a better understanding of the legislative process.

Unfortunately the invitation to research presented by ready access to important data has not been accepted by many scholars. Most empirical studies of legislative voting behavior have been exclusively concerned with the impact of external forces like party discipline and constituency pressure on the legislator's decision. Yet as we have already seen in Chapter One, to ignore completely the role of the legislator's attitudes and presuppositions in the legislative process is to overlook one of its major ingredients. A handful of studies, however, do attempt to demonstrate this systematically and empirically.

The first and still one of the most notable of these studies is Stuart Rice's *Farmers and Workers in American Politics*,[39] published in 1924. In this work Rice demonstrates statistically that state legislators who are farmers or workers have different voting patterns from those following other occupations. The procedure he followed was extremely simple. Determining first of all the occupations of the state legislators, he then devised an index of cohesion which expresses numerically the degree to which groups of two or more legislators vote together. In this case the index number 0 signifies that the group under study displayed no voting cohesion (i.e., voted 50% yea, and 50% nay), and 100 indicates that all the members of the group voted on the same side of all issues. Then the index of cohesion was computed for the two or more parties in the legislature and for the farmers and workers within each party. If being a farmer or a worker had no influence upon the legislator's voting behavior, one would expect the index number of cohesion of the occupational groups to be, over a large number of issues, the same as that of their respective parties. As can be seen in Table 8, this was not the case. Rather the farmers and workers voted with the members of their occupational groups a good deal more often than with the members of their respective parties. It can also be seen that for the legislative sessions studied the workers were somewhat more united than the farmers, that the workers were most agreed on matters directly affecting their economic interests, but the farmers were least agreed on agricultural policy and most agreed on moral questions.

The index of cohesion can also be used to determine the relative cohesion of many groups within a legislature. In Table 9 the relative cohesion on fifteen major issues of selected groups within the United States Senate is presented. It can be seen at a glance that a number of occuptional, religious, and sectional groups were considerably more united in the roll-call voting than the two major parties.

The index of cohesion is not the only means by which voting records of legislators can be analyzed. A simple index of conservatism-liberalism,[40] which has been devised and used in recent years, makes it possible to determine the characteristics of Congressmen with liberal or conservative voting records. The author's analysis of the voting records of the Senators of the 81st Congress

TABLE 8

The Cohesion of Farmers and Workers in State Legislatures

Type of Issue	Farmers Average Difference between Cohesion of Farmers and Cohesion of Their Political Party	Workers Average Difference between Cohesion of Workers and Cohesion of Their Political Party
Prohibition	+22.9	+ 9.6
Sex relationships	+11.0	+15.5
Morals (miscellaneous)	+17.0	− 2.0*
Political reform	+ 8.6	+11.1
Woman suffrage	+ 7.6*	+ 9.3*
Public utilities	+ 6.0	+12.0
Labor	+ 7.7	+23.5
Agriculture	+ 2.7	+18.0
Taxation	+ 6.2	+17.5
Public health	+14.2	+13.8
All issues	+10.2	+15.7
	(1,359 roll calls)	(1,259 roll calls)

* Too few cases for reliable results.

TABLE 9

Relative Cohesion of Selected Groups in the U. S. Senate, 81st Congress, 1st Session

Group	Index of Cohesion
Professors	89
Methodists	54
Easterners	50
Republicans	49
Roman Catholics	49
Southerners	44
Midwesterners	43
Episcopalians	43
Democrats	42
Over 70 years old	38
Entire Membership	28

found, for example, that regardless of party affiliation the younger Senators tended to be more liberal than the older ones; Catholics, more liberal than Protestants; Senators who were immigrants or sons of immigrants, more liberal than those from families with a longer residence in the United States; professional men, more liberal than business men; and the more political experience the Senator possessed, the less likely he was to have either a very liberal or very conservative voting record and the more likely he was to have a middle-of-the-road one.

These facts are presented not to suggest that the identical result necessarily will be obtained by subsequent research but rather to indicate that several different studies using different methods have found a clear relationship between the legislator's social background and his voting record. This does not of course prove that this relationship is necessarily a causal one. Young Senators, for example, may tend to be more liberal than the older ones for reasons other than their age—say, lack of political experience. Similarly Roman Catholics may tend to be liberal not because of their Catholicism but because of something else—ethnic background, for example, or because this type of voting behavior is a condition for political survival in their states. Similarly the farmers that Rice studied may not have voted together so often because of their occupation as because farmers tend to be elected to state legislatures from similar constituencies. The studies made so far indicate only correlation, not cause and effect. More refined methods of analysis are necessary before cause and effect questions can be answered.

Personality and Official Behavior

Almost no systematic research has been undertaken on the relationship between a man's personality and his behavior in public office. Yet there appears to be general agreement among the students in this field that there is a continual interplay or interaction between public office and personality.[41]

The laws, rules, and expectations which define the office shape in very large measure the decisions and actions of its incumbent. But influence also flows the other way—the personality of the incumbent also influences the office itself. Those with either agitator or administrative personalities tend, according to Lasswell, to seek out and be most effective in offices where they may satisfy their dramatic or compulsive tendencies. Yet regardless of the office in which a person finds himself he will tend to emphasize as much as possible that aspect of his job which best fits his personality. Thus the two Roosevelts emphasized the agitational possibilities in the office of President of the United States, and presidents with more administrative-type personalities, such as Calvin Coolidge or Herbert Hoover, stressed the office's administrative opportunities. Lasswell has found the same phenomenon among judges and administrators. This is certainly a beginning, but no more than a beginning, to a probing of the interaction between the office and the person.

chapter four

Political Decision-Makers in Great Britain, Germany, and the Soviet Union

Studies of the social background of American political decision-makers have been essentially static. They suggest very little about the differences in social background of government officials at different times in history. Students of the social background of political decision-makers in other countries, however, have been primarily concerned with discovering such changes. In the following pages we shall look at the historical trends in the governing personnel of Great Britain, Germany, and the Soviet Union.

Great Britain

Political democracy evolved gradually from feudal institutions in England. A powerful, landed aristocracy, which had earlier prevented the development of absolute monarchy, held a virtual monopoly on political power until the nineteenth century. Here quite literally was a ruling class which not only dominated the state but most other institutions as well. During the nineteenth century, however, a number of important changes occurred in British society. Industrialism led to the rise in economic importance of a capitalist middle class and resulted in the formation of an industrial working class. These economic and social changes were paralleled by the spread of democratic ideas and the gradual expansion of the electorate. The twin forces of industrialism and democracy inspired much of the theory in this field. Marx, Weber, Mosca, Pareto, Michels, and those who wrote after them foresaw different resolutions to the conflict of industrialism and democracy with older cultural patterns. The British experience gives us an unusual opportunity to test their speculations against hard facts. What actually was the impact of these forces on the nature of British political personnel?

Trends in the Social Origins of Cabinet Members

The consequences of industrialism and democracy for Cabinet personnel can be seen at a glance in Table 10. Clearly the old exclusiveness of the Cabinet broke down. Within a century of the Reform Act of 1832, which granted suffrage to some of the middle class for the first time, the Cabinet had become

TABLE 10

Class Origins of Members of the British Cabinet, 1801–1935
(In Percentages)

Cabinet	Year	Aristocracy	Middle Class	Working Class	Total	
(Average)	1801–31	73	27	0	100	(71)
(Average)	1832–66	64	36	0	100	(100)
(Average)	1867–84	60	40	0	100	(58)
Gladstone	1886	60	40	0	100	(15)
Salisbury	1886	67	33	0	100	(15)
Gladstone	1892	53	47	0	100	(17)
Salisbury	1895	42	58	0	100	(19)
Balfour	1902	47	53	0	100	(19)
Campbell-Bannerman	1906	37	58	5	100	(19)
Asquith	1914	32	63	5	100	(19)
Lloyd George	1919	14	81	5	100	(21)
Bonar Law	1922	50	50	0	100	(16)
MacDonald	1924	16	26	58	100	(19)
Baldwin	1925	43	57	0	100	(21)
MacDonald	1929	11	22	67	100	(18)
National Ministry	1935	33	56	11	100	(18)

dominated by the middle class. But perhaps the most noteworthy feature of the British experience was the slowness with which the background of Cabinet personnel changed. There was a substantial lag, amounting to the better part of a century, between the time the middle class became dominant in the electorate and the time it became dominant in the Cabinet. A similar time lag between the achievement of electoral power and Cabinet representation can be observed for the working class. Even today the aristocracy has by no means been routed and still enjoys a representation in the British Cabinet quite out of line with its numerical size. Why this long delay before dominant electoral groups become governing groups? Why the vestige of aristocratic power in this day of the welfare state?

There are a number of probable explanations for the time-lag phenomenon. The first and most platitudinous is the conservatism of the British electorate. It no doubt takes some time before a previously disenfranchised group begins voting for their own kind in Britain or any other country. This perhaps accounts for the fact that the middle class were not dominant in the House of Commons immediately after the electoral reforms. But an even longer time lag—actually 30 or 40 years[1]—occurred between the time when middle-class Members of Parliament became common and their entry in force into the Cabinet. The principal reason for this seems to be that an M.P. does not ordinarily become a member of a Cabinet until he has served a substantial apprenticeship as "back-bencher" and junior minister. This obviously means that a new group, entering Parliament for the first time, cannot expect to be represented in the Cabinet for perhaps ten or twenty years. Thus the British parliamentary system greatly slows down this type of response to political change and indoctrinates new leadership groups in the rules of the game for many years before they are intrusted with supreme power. But if this apprenticeship period were the only factor involved in the lag between representation in the House and in the Cabinet, one would expect, once the initial apprenticeship period was completed, that the personnel of the Cabinet and the personnel of the House of Commons would be very much the same. The fact of the matter is that the backgrounds of the members of the Cabinet and the Parliament are far from being the same.

Cabinet Recruitment within the House of Commons

In Table 11 the social backgrounds of Cabinet members and M.P.s are

TABLE 11

Social Backgrounds of British Cabinet Members Compared to the House of Commons
(In Percentages)

	Cabinet	House
Parentage	*1918–35*	*1918–35*
Aristocrats	23	13
Commoners	77	87
Education	*1917–24*	*1918–24*
Public School	56	55
Oxford	35	16
Cambridge	17	13
Other university	8	13
Total with university training	60	42
Occupation	*1916–35*	*1918–35*
Agriculture (includes land owning)	14	2
Rentiers (not gainfully employed)	12	10
Business (commerce, finance, industry, transport)	11	37
Civil and military service	5	11
Professional	44	35
All others (includes trade unions & party officials, manual labor)	14	4

compared for the period immediately preceding World War II. The slightly different categories and time periods used in the three different studies from which the table has been constructed make it not entirely satisfactory for our purposes. But even if one allows for these shortcomings, it is clear that the Cabinet was at that time a more exclusive body than the House of Commons. There was a larger proportion of members of titled families, graduates of public schools or of Oxford and Cambridge, and landowners, rentiers, and professional men in the Cabinet than in the House during this period.

There seem to be several factors involved in an explanation of this fact. Since to this very day parliamentary salaries are too small to support a member unless he has some other source of income, this means that many politically ambitious men do not find it possible to stand for Parliament until rather late in life. The politically ambitious man with some measure of financial security obtained early in life, however, can enter Parliament at a much earlier age. He has a far better chance of serving a ten- or twenty-year apprenticeship usually necessary for a Cabinet post than the man who enters Parliament only upon retirement. Thus the internal selecting mechanism of the House of Commons by favoring the man elected early in life favors the man with inherited means and also the professional men (especially barristers and journalists) who can combine a political and an occupational career. The active businessman finds this combination as difficult in Britain as in America. Civil servants and officers in the armed services fairly often stand for seats in the House of Commons, but normally cannot do so until after their retirement. Thus the race for Cabinet seats is far from an equal one but rather favors those who can begin a political career early in life.

A final factor explaining why the Cabinet is more aristocratic and exclusive than the Commons should be mentioned. During most of British history the nation has been ruled by a tiny group of "kings, lords and gentlemen,"[2] and for the most part they have ruled responsibly and well. They have set the tone and style of British politics in the past, and even the most cursory examination shows that much of the old noblesse-oblige tradition still holds today. In such a political milieu those who have learned the rules of the game from early life, who go to the "right" schools and universities will often have a political advantage over those who have not had such benefits. And, until recently at least, a certain cliquishness has had some influence over the choice of Cabinet officers. It could hardly be a coincidence that Lord Balfour, an old Etonian, selected almost half of his Cabinet from the Eton men in the House; and that Mr. Baldwin, a Harrow graduate, had in his government the largest number of Harrovians ever collected in a single Cabinet.[3] Finally, the British aristocracy has shown unparalleled ability to absorb disparate groups—business tycoon or successful politician today, a Lord tomorrow. This ability to bring into the aristocracy those successful in business and politics has had an enervating effect on the aristocracy and a debilitating effect on the political power of other strata of society. It has also meant that many groups have found sympathetic leaders among the aristocracy to press for the attainment of their wishes.

We began this section by asking why the ascent of middle- and working-class elements into the Cabinet was so gradual in Great Britain. A number of reasons have been suggested: first, some lag between the time these groups obtained suffrage and began voting for their own kind; second, the requirement in the parliamentary system for a fairly long period of apprenticeship in the House before a Cabinet post is achieved; third, that the selection of Cabinet members from within the House favors those with either independent means or occupations that can be combined with parliamentary service; and fourth, the openness and responsible behavior of the British aristocracy. All of these factors have greatly retarded a growth in representation of middle- and working-class groups in the Cabinet. There is one further factor to be considered: the unrepresentative nature of the House of Commons itself.

The People, Parties, and the House of Commons

The essential facts for the House elected in 1945 are presented in Table 12. Even in this House, which possessed a large Labor Party majority, almost one out of every ten members was born in a titled family (even more were aristocrats by creation or marriage), over 40% had attended the public schools, 30% had attended Oxford or Cambridge, and over 50% were professional men. Since comparable figures are not available for the whole adult population, it is impossible to say with accuracy just how unrepresentative this Commons really was. However, during the interwar period, 1918–1935, Ross made the

TABLE 12

Social Backgrounds of the House of Commons, by Party, 1945
(In Percentages)

	Conservative	Labor	Total*
Parentage			
Aristocrats	21	1	8
Commoners	79	99	92
	100	100	100
School			
Elementary	2	53	34
Secondary	13.5	24	21.5
Public	84.5	23	44.5
	100	100	100
University			
Did not attend	41	68	58
Attended	59	32	42
Oxford	(29)	(9)	(17)
Cambridge	(20)	(5)	(11)
Other	(12)	(21)	(18)
	100**	100**	100**
Occupational Status			
Professions	61	48.5	53.5
Employers and managers	32.5	9.5	17.5
Workers	3	41	27
Unoccupied (includes housewife)	3.5	1	2
	100	100	100
	(n=215)	(n=401)	(n=640)

* Includes Liberals, etc.
** Apparent discrepancies are due to the fact that some members attended more than one university.

estimates of the differences in political opportunities of various groups summarized below:[4]

Those who had attended secondary school (5% of the population) had 18 times the average chance of becoming an M.P.
Public school graduates (2% of the population) had 115 times the average chance of becoming an M.P.: a Harrow boy, 1800; and an Eton boy, 2000 times the average chance.
A Cambridge man had 140 times, and an Oxford man 180 times the average chance of becoming an M.P.
Professional men had 12 times the chance, employers and managers 6 times the chance, and the unoccupied 3 times the average chance of becoming an M.P.

Since the prewar period, the House of Commons has become slightly more representative of the electorate, so that the differences in political opportunities figured by Ross are probably not quite so high today. Even so it is clear that in Great Britain as well as in America those ranking near the top of the society's system of stratification possess the best political opportunities.

The second thing to be observed in Table 12 is the substantial differences in social background between the members of the two parliamentary parties. Over 20% of the Conservative M.P.s were born in titled families; only 1% of the Laborites were so fortunate. Eighty-five per cent of the Conservatives attended public schools; only 23% of the Laborites did, and so on. The figures establish beyond all doubt the strong class basis of the leadership of the two major parties.*

Perhaps the most interesting fact in the table is that 27% of the total members of Parliament and 41% of the Laborites are workers. As we have already seen, workers are almost nonexistent among American political decision-makers. How can this figure be explained? Does this refute our original hypothesis that political leaders tend to be chosen from near the top of a society's system of stratification?

The first thing to note about the workers in Parliament is that most of them are also trade-union officials.[5] This makes their position in society rather difficult to assess, for they may be actual manual workers who more or less incidentally have been officials of their unions, or they may be men who have made trade-union organization a life work. Certainly to call men like Ernest Bevin, Aneurin Bevan, or Herbert Morrison workers is as unrealistic as it would be to call John L. Lewis a miner or Walter Reuther an auto worker in the United States. It seems safe to assume that a large number if not most of the workers in the House of Commons have not practiced their original trade for some years; and though they originated in and speak for the workers, they are today more aptly described as administrators, journalists, and politicians.

But even if this be true, the fact that 27% of the House of Commons in 1945 were workers or trade-union officials is highly significant. Paradoxically the more rigid and inequalitarian British society seems to have a larger proportion of the working class in positions of political authority than the more mobile and open society of the United States. How can this paradox be explained?

In Great Britain the fairly rigid class structure has resulted in a substantial degree of class consciousness and solidarity. This has contributed to the development of trade unions to the point at which some of them are among the biggest and most important organizations both economically and politically in the country. The top-level jobs in the union movement in Great Britain call for political and managerial skills and ability of a high order. And these jobs are open only to those with working-class origins and at least some experience as rank-and-file workers. Thus the union movement in Britain has provided a new channel of upward mobility open exclusively to those whose opportunities for advancement in other fields of endeavor are slight.

Another factor needs to be considered. When class lines are clearly drawn and class identification is strong, party politics is likely to be conducted along

---

* The House of Commons elected in 1945 is not altogether typical. Since the safest Labor Party seats go to the trade unionists and the safest Conservative seats generally go to wealthy upper-class members, the landslide victory for the Labor Party resulted in the Parliamentary Conservative Party being unusually aristocratic and the Parliamentary Labor Party more middle-class in background than usual. The available data on later Houses is not as satisfactory as that for 1945, thus 1945 figures have been used despite their distortion which is not in any event great enough to change the general picture.

class lines. Once in politics, the union leaders discovered that the job of trade-union official combines fairly well with that of politician and Member of Parliament. The unions supplement the M.P.s salary (which is inadequate even for those habituated to a modest scale of living), provide necessary funds for political compaigning and an alternative occupation in case of defeat.*

We have mentioned earlier in discussing the background of elected officials in the United States that the electorate seems to be torn between voting for someone like themselves or for someone who represents what they would like to be. In Great Britain the union leader can in a sense satisfy both of these desires for the working-class voter. The union leader is "one of us" at least in his origins. And since in Britain the level of aspiration of members of the working class is far lower than in the United States, the union official is also considered by many voters to be a successful man. In the United States definitions of success tend to be about the same for all classes. The successful man to the American worker is more likely to be a professional man or a businessman than a union leader or official, even though the American worker's objective chances of obtaining such a goal are quite low.

Thus we find the paradox of the more equalitarian of the two societies having fewer members of the lower social strata among its political decision-makers than the more rigid and class-bound society.[6]

Germany

While British politics has been characterized by stability and gradual change, Germany has had a quite different history. In Germany social stability has been combined with extreme political instability. The basic causes of political instability in Germany are complex and subject to much debate. We need not enter into this controversy here. Our concern with Germany is limited to probing the connection between political instability and the nature of Germany's governing personnel. Fortunately two Hoover Institute studies provide us with some relevant data on this question.

Cabinet Members under the Monarchy, the Republic, and the Nazis

Maxwell Knight's *The German Executive*[7] is a study of the members of the German cabinet from 1890 to 1945. This cabinet not only was called by different names under the monarchy (1890–1918) and during the Wiemar (1918–1933) and Nazi (1933–1945) periods, but also possessed a quite different constitutional position. In imperial Germany the nearest thing to cabinet officers were the *Staats-Sekretäre* who were strictly administrative officers responsible to the Kaiser. Under the Wiemar Republic the cabinet became a political body responsible to the Reichstag (legislature) through the Federal Chancellor. Under Hitler the cabinet once again reverted to a purely technical, bureaucratic organization which implemented, rather than made, public policy. As a result of these constitutional changes, the cabinet members during these three periods are not strictly comparable groups of men. Yet changes in their

---

* During the early years of the Labor Party many elderly trade-union officials were "retired" to the House of Commons, a practice which was and still is poor politics. Given the vital importance of an early entry into the House for an M.P.'s chances of becoming a Cabinet member, and the fact that trade-union officials usually possess the safest Labor Party seats, it is clear that it is to the interests of the unions to encourage young union leaders to enter Parliament.

social backgrounds may none the less provide some clues to the changing composition of the German political elite.

The trends in the social backgrounds of German cabinet members are quite different from those of their British counterparts. In England, as we have already seen, there was a gradual opening of the Cabinet to middle-class and working-class elements. In Germany somewhat similar changes also occurred but more abruptly. As a consequence there were rather sharp differences between the cabinet members who served in the imperial, Wiemar, and Nazi periods. There was, for instance, a substantial shift in the class origins of cabinet members during these three eras (see Table 13). During the monarchy

TABLE 13

Class Background of Members of the German Cabinet, 1890–1945
(In Percentages)

Class	Monarchy 1890–1918	Republic 1918–1933	Nazi 1933–1945
Aristocracy	64.5	11.5	27
Middle class	35.5	78	70
Labor	0	11	3
	100	100.5	100

the cabinet was overwhelmingly aristocratic in background; under the Wiemar Republic, almost exclusively middle-class with a small minority of its members coming up from the working class through the labor movement. But—and here the counterrevolutionary nature of the Nazi movement becomes very clear—the Nazis actually reversed the trend toward more middle- and working-class cabinet members.

The shifts in the structure of the cabinet during these three eras can be seen in more detail in Table 14. It is clear that during all of these periods the occu-

TABLE 14

All Nonpolitical Occupations of German Cabinet Members, 1890–1945
(In Percentages)

Occupational Groups	Monarchy 1890–1918	Republic 1918–1933	Nazi 1933–1945
Civil service	64.5	48	48.5
Military service	17	7	18
Professions	47	65	45
Business	5	19	39
Farming	3	7	12
Clerical & sales	1	4	6
Labor	3	11	3

pational distribution within the cabinet is by no means a direct reflection of the distribution of power in German society. Under the monarchy, for instance, the extremely powerful Junker (landowning) and business groups are hardly represented at all in the cabinet, perhaps being, as Paul Kecskemeti suggests in his introduction to Knight's book, certain enough of their power to be content with political representation through sympathetic political agents like civil servants and lawyers.[8] But even if one takes this important factor into consideration, it is likely that changes in the nonpolitical occupations of the cabinet reflect to some extent changes in the balance of power within German society. The establishment of the Wiemar Republic and the changing of the cabinet into a political body resulted in a decline of the civil servant and professional military man in the cabinet. The middle-class professional men—lawyers, journalists, teachers—began to provide the bulk of the cabinet members. The lower-ranking occupational groups—clerical and manual workers—also began to provide a minority of political decision-makers. The Nazi revolution changed the cabinet back into a bureaucratic body. As a result, the professional men, whose great importance in democratic politics has already been demonstrated, declined in numbers until they were actually slightly less numerous than under the monarchy. (Within the professional group the lawyers and journalists were hardest hit.) The same thing happened to the small manual-labor group. On the other hand, the proportion of military men in the cabinet made a strong comeback under the Nazis while businessmen, clerical and sales workers, and farmers continued to increase their representation. Thus the triumph of Nazism resulted in a partial return to the imperial pattern of bureaucratic-military dominance of the cabinet. But under the Nazis these older elements were combined with an increased representation for business and agrarian groups.

Probably the most important other differences in the backgrounds of cabinet members during these three periods were political. The degree of circulation and change in personnel within the cabinet progressed from great stability under the monarchy to rapid turnover during the Wiemar Republic to virtual stagnation during the Nazi period. (The average tenure of cabinet members in each period was 43.5, 7.7 and 79 months respectively.)[9] Similarly the type of political experience possessed by cabinet members varied in the three periods. Under the monarchy the cabinet was composed primarily of former bureaucrats; under the Wiemar Republic it was composed of politicians who had previously served in elective office; and under the Nazis there were two principal channels to the cabinet: the Nazi Party and the civil service. Thus under the Nazis the cabinet became a strange mixture of Nazi demagogues and nonpolitical career administrators.

Revolution and the Social Backgrounds of Cabinet Members

Perhaps the most significant findings in Knight's study of the German cabinet are not the differences between the imperial, Wiemar, and Nazi periods but the changes in background within each period. In the crisis period immediately preceding the Revolution of 1918 an abnormally large number of persons without previous cabinet experience became cabinet members. A similar rapid interjection of new blood occurred immediately preceding the Nazi revolution. The frequency with which new personnel entered the cabinet is expressed graphically in the diagram. These new inexperienced cabinet ministers who served shortly before the two revolutions tended to be older men who had made substantial reputations outside of politics. Thus the age and nonpolitical accomplishments of the cabinet as a whole also show a wave-like pattern, going up rapidly immediately before the revolution and dropping

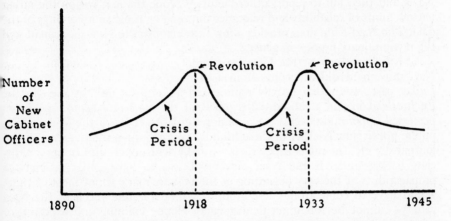

off rapidly as a result of the subsequent change in regime. Furthermore the new men drawn into the cabinet immediately before the revolutions had some of the characteristics of the persons who eventually deposed them.

It seems likely that in these periods of political crisis and threatened revolution the ruling regime, in an attempt to stabilize the situation, drew in some outside, nonpolitical persons enjoying wide prestige who had not been closely identified with the discredited regime. These men seemed to be chosen so as to have some of the characteristics and style of the most powerful threatening groups, thus to divert and weaken them. Both Mosca and Pareto have argued that ruling groups, if they are to maintain political stability, must be able to absorb the leaders of alternative groups that threaten their position. The English experience indicates how this can be done. But in Germany the ruling groups were perhaps too ingrown, too well entrenched to show the requisite flexibility. Once the revolutionary crisis had begun a last-minute effort was made to change. In Knight's words ". . . the dam leaked before it completely burst."[10] In both cases, however, these efforts came too late to avoid the destruction of the regime.

Nazi Leaders: Alienation and Marginality

Daniel Lerner's study of The Nazi Elite[11] provides a closer look at one set of revolutionary leaders in recent German history.

This study is based entirely upon the biographical sketches contained in the 1934 Fuehrerlexikon, a Who's Who of Nazism. While this procedure has the advantage of concentrating attention upon the Nazi movement during its revolutionary stage, it also has serious drawbacks. The Fuehrerlexikon contains the biographies of a number of men who were neither sympathetic to nor active in the movement but who, because of their prominence, the Nazis found convenient to claim as adherents. And this reliance upon a single reference work results in a failure to obtain significant data for a large number of the subjects of the study. Conclusions drawn upon the basis of information for sometimes less than half the total sample are subject to a very wide margin of error, an error which might have been reduced through consulting other sources. Further, semiofficial reference works of this sort are certain to emphasize accomplishments and characteristics that were considered "good" by the

Nazis, but then fail to report other factors.[12] None the less, within the rather narrow limits of reliability and relevance imposed by these shortcomings of the data, *The Nazi Elite* does provide a few insights into the Nazi movement and the revolutionary process in general.

As Knight's study of the German cabinet suggests, the leadership of the Nazi movement did not come from a single strata of German society. The *Junker* caste was rather heavily represented among the military men in the *Fuehrerlexikon* and a substantial segment of the Nazi propaganda specialists possessed upper-middle-class backgrounds similar to those of the Wiemar Republic politicians. Neither of these findings is startling—military men, editors, journalists, etc., in pre-Nazi Germany usually had upper- and upper-middle-class backgrounds. If the Nazi movement was to have either generals or propagandists at the very beginning of the regime, many if not most of them would have to come from these groups. A modern state—even of the Nazi variety—cannot be run upon demagoguery alone. Training and expertise of some middle-class professional men are essential. But in addition to the military men and propaganda specialists the Nazi leadership contained a far larger group of what Lerner calls "plebeian" administrators. Upon closer examination it is evident that the plebeian label given this group is rather misleading, for they were primarily petit-bourgeois or rural lower-class in background. It is this group along with the leaders of the political police that increased their social status most by means of the Nazi revolution. They tended to join the movement earliest and to rise the highest within the movement.

It should be emphasized that the differences in pre-Nazi social position of the Nazi military men, propagandists, administrators, and policemen were often quite small. Further, each group contained a very wide spread or deviation from the norm. But Lerner's analysis points out that there were tendencies, often slight, for those with different skills and roles within the Nazi movement to have different social backgrounds. It also points out that the Nazi leadership came in significant numbers from *all* classes in German society except one: the urban working class. What brought these rather disparate elements together into a common opposition to the Wiemar Republic and a common commitment to Nazism? Lerner's analysis suggests two factors, *alienation* and *marginality*.

Alienation, originally a Marxian concept, has come to have psychological overtones. *Disaffection* is perhaps an approximate synonym. This feeling according to Lerner explains the actions of the minority of upper- and upper-middle-class persons found in the Nazi leadership. In his own words:

. . . the Nazi Propagandists were, characteristically, a class of intellectuals born and raised within the *elite* of Imperial and Wiemar Germany who became *alienated* from the prevailing structure of symbols and sanctions of the elite which nurtured them.[13]

The data used in the study of the Nazi elite is neither of the right sort nor available in sufficient quantity or quality to explain how or why this alienation took place. The intellectuals in the *Fuehrerlexicon* seemed to have experienced a high level of unemployment although the nature of the data makes this conclusion almost entirely speculation.[14] Similarly it is suggested that the Nazi military leaders became alienated after the restriction of the German armed forces with the loss of their career opportunities as a result of the Treaty of Versailles. About the most that can be said for all this is that the alienation of many intellectual and professional men from the Wiemar institutions and democratic values was no doubt one factor in the rise of the Nazi Party. The data on the careers of Nazi leaders found in the Lerner study does not (and perhaps could not) demonstrate the existence of alienation. Social background data is of rather limited usefulness in serving as an index for the existence of such a psychological condition.

The second explanation offered by Lerner is *marginality*. This concept is almost the exact opposite of alienation. The alienated man is one who has emotionally withdrawn from something, in this case from his commitment to the values and the way of life of the Wiemar upper-middle class. The marginal man, on the other hand, is one who has never belonged. He is a man who is not a part of the dominant cultural pattern, like the professor in a "Business Civilization," a Jew in a Christian land, or a Negro in a white society. Such a social position, it is widely believed, makes one especially vulnerable to revolutionary and fanatical political appeals. ". . . The Nazi movement was led and followed by marginal men."[15]

In substantiation of this conclusion Lerner discovered that 78% of the propagandists, 82% of the administrators, 77% of the policemen and 51% of the military men found in the *Fuehrerlexicon* were marginal in one or more ways. Considerable doubt is cast upon these figures, however, by the indexes of marginality used in the study.[16] For example, foreign birth or birth in Alsace-Lorraine, the Saar, or the Rhineland were considered marginal characteristics. This seems plausible. But Catholicism is hardly marginal in the Catholic southwest of Germany where the Nazi movement began. No consideration is taken of this fact. Similarly, being the son of a peasant or artisan or having been married before age 21 or having been an enlisted man in World War I or being a graduate of a grade school without further education, etc., hardly seem to be marginal characteristics; yet they are counted as such. Again *The Nazi Elite* falls into the trap of using analytical concepts for which adequate indexes cannot be devised from the available data. That the leaders of the Nazi movement tended to be marginal men or alienated men are both interesting hypotheses. Despite the data and interpretation of *The Nazi Elite* they still remain unproved hypotheses.

The Soviet Union

While the facts about German political decision-makers provide some insights into the origins and dynamics of revolutionary movements, the limited amount of factual information on the backgrounds of the leaders of the Soviet Union suggests that substantial changes occur within a revolutionary movement once it becomes consolidated in power.

While a number of scattered studies of Soviet leaders exist, the most germane is George K. Schueller's study of the members of the Politburo of the Communist Party of the Soviet Union.[17] While the dozen or so men who serve in the Politburo (now called the Presidium) at one time do not comprise all of the top-level decision-makers in the Soviet Union, an analysis of the trends in the social backgrounds of these men should provide us with a reasonably accurate picture of the changes in the entire Soviet leadership group since 1917.

Career Patterns of Politburo Members during the Leninist Period

It has become a commonplace that the Russian Revolution of 1917 was not led by workers or peasants but by middle-class intellectuals. Lenin, Trotsky, and most of the other members of the Politburo in the early years of the Soviet Union were well educated, cosmopolitan revolutionists. Schueller has summarized the "typical" career patterns of the early members of the Politburo as follows:[18]

> Born in a town or metropolis
> Of middle-class origins
> Joins the Communist Party at an early age, but probably after 20
> Probably attends a university
> Does propaganda work for the Party
> Is arrested and jailed several times
> Goes abroad; studies and writes there
> Returns to Russia and participates in the Revolution
> Becomes a member of the Party Central Committee
> Becomes an important government official
> Becomes a member of the Politburo

Thus once again we see the crucial importance of the intellectual as the spearhead of revolution. It should be noticed that the backgrounds of the members of the Politburo indicate that the Russian Revolution of 1917, unlike the German revolutions of 1918 and 1933, resulted in a complete break with the past. While the leaders of the Russian revolution were for the most part born in comfortable middle-class conditions, their pre-1917 revolutionary activity had made them "criminals" and "outlaws" in Czarist society.

From the death of Lenin in 1924 until Stalin's consolidation of his position after the purges in 1937, the Politburo and the top leadership of the Soviet Union were in a transitional stage. But those members of the Politburo with middle-class-intellectual-cosmopolitan backgrounds proved to be ". . . Stalin's main targets of internecine violence among the Soviet elite."[19]

Career Patterns of Politburo Members during the Stalinist Period

As a result, the "typical" career pattern of a Politburo member from 1938 until the death of Stalin became quite different. Schueller summarizes the Stalinist Politburo member's background as follows:[20]

> Born in a village
> Of low social origin
> Joins Party before the age of 20
> Does Party work in trouble spots like the Ukraine or the Caucasus; also does some police work
> Has no higher education
> Becomes a member of the Party Central Committee
> Becomes a member of the Secretariat
> Becomes a candidate to the Politburo
> High government job
> Member of the Politburo

The urban, middle-class, professional revolutionaries were replaced by relatively uneducated bureaucrats and party organizers with peasant backgrounds

The Soviet experience suggests that while it may take intellectuals to make a revolution, a total state does not for long remain out of the hands of the bureaucrats. With this shift in the career patterns of the Soviet leaders has gone a slowing down of the original revolutionary dynamism and a deflection of the regime from the wholehearted pursuit of some of its original goals. Policies of nationalism, wide wage differentials, protecting the sanctity of marriage, etc. which the bureaucratic leaders of the Soviet Union have initiated may be practical but they are also reactionary in the chronological sense of the word.[21] And since bureaucracy is a form of organization based on an extreme division of labor and specialization of function—with the resultant wide differences in social prestige and status—the Soviet example shows that the quest for absolute political equality through totalitarian means is not only incompatible with freedom but also self-defeating. The rigid stratification of the Czarist period has been replaced by the new bureaucratic stratification of Stalin and Malenkov.[22] This extreme bureaucratization may, in the long run, be self-defeating in yet another way. The total subordination of the intellectual to the bureaucrat may result in eventual destruction of the regime through the failure to provide for the expansion and application of organized knowledge to the problems of governance. The man of knowledge performs an essential social and political function which cannot be performed if he is turned into an automaton.[23] In this respect, too, the total bureaucratized state eventually may prove to be self-defeating.

chapter five

Theories and Facts: A Comparative Analysis

The time has come to sum up. What have we learned from this review of the existing literature on the social backgrounds of political decision-makers?

Areas of Knowledge

Both the theories and facts analyzed in the preceding chapters point to rather definite conclusions about the recruitment of political decision-makers. They also suggest a number of more debatable inferences about political stability and revolution.

Recruitment of Decision-Makers

First of all, political decision-makers are not a cross section of the society, not ". . . an average sample of ordinary men."[1] While the exact picture varies from society to society and from time to time, we have found that they tend to come from near the top of the society's system of social stratification. The Marxists, believing that the state is but the executive committee of the dominant economic class, find these facts compatible with their views. The right-wing prophets of the inevitability of political domination by some form of elite do also. But both the Marxists and the elitists overlook the fact that a group or class need not be literally represented among decision-makers, at least under democratic conditions, in order to have political power or to have it exercised in their behalf. As long as sympathetic agents of a group or class can achieve high public office, actual members of the group need not.

Why does this tendency to select decision-makers from among those with relatively high prestige positions prevail? We have suggested several reasons. The individual who enjoys relatively high social status has attained success according to the society's definition. He is likely to be considered a better man than those who have not acquired the symbols of success. Furthermore, the financial resources, free time, and motivation necessary to achieve high elective office are most often possessed by those with relatively high social status. It should not be forgotten in this connection that Aristotle characterized popular election as an essentially oligarchical device. Finally, opportunities to obtain the requisite special training and skills needed to fill technical (civil service) offices are far from equal. As a consequence of these and perhaps other factors we have seen that there are substantial inequalities in political life-chances in the societies which we have studied. As a result, political decision-makers are unrepresentative in their backgrounds.

One should be careful not to push this conclusion too far. True, the tendency for political opportunities to increase as one climbs the social ladder is very real, but this does not mean that all decision-makers are of one class, or are necessarily an extremely homogeneous group. In the United States, Great Britain, and Germany we found that the decision-makers, as well as we can tell from not entirely complete or satisfactory data, have been a fairly heterogeneous group despite this tendency. The leaders of the Soviet Union were probably the most homogeneous in their backgrounds of any group we have analyzed. Furthermore the data on decision-makers in England and Germany show that they as a group can and do become somewhat more representative, more like "an average sample of ordinary men" under certain conditions. Interestingly enough, this seems to have occurred to a far larger extent in the more class-bound societies with democratic political institutions such as England and Wiemar Germany than in the United States. It would seem that in a fairly rigid class system, such as England's or Germany's, the voter more often prefers to be literally represented by an actual member of his class than is true in the more open society of the United States. And of course a more class-bound society is likely to have class-based political parties and a politically active trade-union movement which together supply an avenue to high public office for a few members of the working class.

Secondly, it is clear that a great deal more than relatively high social status is required in order to become a political decision-maker. We have seen that other social requirements—age, sex, residence, etc.—often have as great influence on political opportunities as the class structure. Also the demands of some high-status positions—those of physicians and engineers, for example—seem largely incompatible with political activity and hence supply relatively few decision-makers in democratic nations. And, perhaps most important of all, an individual must have the desire, skill, and endurance necessary to succeed in a political career before he can expect to become a decision-maker. Knowledge about the motivations and skills of decision-makers is almost nonexistent. But it seems probable that one frequent motivation for a political career is the extreme demand for deference resulting from personal insecurity and a low esteem of the self. And in democratic politics ability at verbal manipulation and group negotiation seems to have characterized the top-level officials. In the two totalitarian systems studied, Nazi Germany and the Soviet Union, the skills of top officials seem to be broadly administrative (including the skills for military and police positions) although skill in propaganda-making was also rather frequent among the Nazi leaders.

The findings on the recruitment of decision-makers, then, are probably more adequate than those on any other aspect of our subject. Yet only a beginning to a complete understanding of this phenomenon has been made. The existing studies, however, do suggest that three factors are involved in the development of a political decision-maker:

1. Social structure influences political opportunities
2. Personality structure supplies political motivation
3. Political skills influence the degree of political success

By further research on the relationship between these three factors and political accomplishment, a more adequate picture of the selection of decision-makers may eventually be achieved.

Decision-Makers, Revolution, and Social Change

The second major aspect of our subject in which some relatively firm knowledge exists is the relationship between the backgrounds of political decision-makers and social, economic, and political change.

In studying decision-makers in Great Britain we saw how the change from an essentially feudal society to a modern, industrial, democratic society was reflected in the backgrounds of her top-level government officials. Through a long, slow, and gradual process the members and agents of the new political forces were admitted to the points of decision. We suggested that the slowness of this process was a result of such factors as the conservatism of the electorate, the long apprenticeship which must be served in the House of Commons before an M.P. becomes eligible for Cabinet office, the advantage of the man with a secure social and financial position over the man who must earn his own way while in politics, and the amazing ability of the British aristocracy to absorb disparate elements. But no matter how slowly this change occurred, the British aristocracy was flexible enough and responsive enough to new forces that abrupt and violent political upheavals were avoided. The British experience provides more than a little documentation to both Pareto's and Mosca's conclusion that a "circulation of the elite" is necessary to achieve political stability.

The importance of this feature of British political development becomes apparent when the British experience is compared with the German. Political instability in Germany has been associated with sudden and fairly radical changes in the backgrounds of her political decision-makers. This suggests that new groups pressing for membership in the organs of state power achieved their goal suddenly. In Pareto's words there has not been a steady and gradual "circulation of the elite" in Germany. Rather, access to positions of political power has tended to be closed to both members and agents of new political groups until immediately before a revolution. In the crises preceding the revolutions of 1918 and 1933 the new power seekers suddenly received some recognition from the older regime, but too late to head off revolutionary change.

Finally, a comparison of the backgrounds of Nazi and Soviet leaders suggests the tremendous importance of middle-class intellectuals and professional men in the revolutionary process. Their skills are essential both to revolutionary political movements and to stable governments. They are also in a position to serve as agents or representatives of less favored groups. In a sense intellectuals and professional men are in the important swing position. Unless a substantial number of them somehow and for some reason become disaffected revolutionaries, there seems to be relatively little danger of revolution. If, on the other hand, their loyalties, beliefs, and interests begin to diverge sharply from established political institutions and values, then the revolutionary dynamism may have been set in motion. But if the Soviet experience is any guide, it seems that in the modern totalitarian state it is the bureaucrats who eventually win in the struggle for power.

None of these remarks should be considered anything but tentative and partial explanations of political instability and revolution. These studies tell us almost nothing about the motivations of revolutionaries. It is also clear that the social backgrounds of political decision-makers are far from being an infallible guide to the distribution of power. The lack of intellectuals among the leaders of the Soviet Union, for example, may not mean that intellectuals have been suppressed, just as the virtual absence of working-class members in the United States does not mean that they are being exploited. It seems likely, however, that in a totalitarian political system the social backgrounds of decision-makers are a better index to the distribution of political power than in democracies.

Areas of Ignorance

Despite the general conclusions drawn above, very little is known about the social backgrounds of decision-makers and their political significance.

Factual Gaps

In part this ignorance is the result of a lack of facts. In the United States the relevant facts are most plentiful for administrators and state legislators but are woefully lacking for other often more important groups such as Senators, Congressmen, Cabinet members (of both kitchen and official varieties), to say nothing of the leaders of political parties and interest groups.[2] Further, studies which attempt to determine historical trends in the characteristics of public officials are almost nonexistent for the United States, yet this type of study is about all that has been done for foreign countries. Curiously enough, a major gap in the facts concerns the *political career patterns* of decision-makers. For the United States, especially, it would be useful to know the usual pattern or sequence of public offices leading to the Presidency or Congress and whether or not there are differences between political career patterns in one-party or two-party areas, between the career patterns of Democrats and Republicans, and so on. Questions such as these have yet to be systematically explored. Finally the facts about the social backgrounds of political decision-makers have been most effective in demonstrating the existence of blocks to access to public office and in explaining why most people are *not* decision-makers rather than why a few people are. Many more facts about the personality structure, motivations, and skills of politically successful people are needed before this can be adequately explained.

Relationship between Theory and Research

The greatest weakness of research in this field has not been a lack of facts but the disparity between theory and empirical research. Perhaps most of the factual studies have fallen into the trap of undirected and crude empiricism. One article, for example, is prefaced by the remark that

. . . the widespread interest in occupations [of state legislators] which the literature reveals seems to justify an extended analysis here, even though there be severe limitations on the reliability of data and *sharp doubt that conclusions which may be drawn will be of social significance.*[3]

It seems to have been often assumed by the researchers in this field that any and all facts take on great significance when displayed in imposing tables of figures worked out to two decimal places. One always is impressed by the industry, patience, and arithmetical skill which have gone into constructing these tables, but not always by their political significance.

The crushing retort to much research on social backgrounds has been "So what?" This query can be answered; there are many ways in which social background data is of great significance to political scientists. But the random collection of facts from *Who's Who* or whatever other source of facts happens to be available will not automatically be significant to political scientists. Rather the collection and interpretation of facts must be guided by theory. For the most part, however, empirical research on the social backgrounds of political decision-makers has not been guided or influenced by theoretical concerns.

The blame for the lack of connection between theory and research in this field should not be attributed exclusively to the fact collectors. The theorists have contributed to it too. Most of the theory has been concerned with demonstrating the inevitability of elites or ruling classes in all political systems. If by this the theorists mean to demonstrate that a political division of labor is necessary in social life, the point is self-evident. Even the direct democracy of the Greek city state or the New England town meeting could not operate without political leadership. But Pareto, Mosca, Michels, and many others meant to imply that the leaders, be they called *elites* or *ruling classes*, were dominant and largely or entirely uncontrollable. These conclusions seem harsh to democratic ears and, as the analysis in Chapter Two suggests, also seem unwarranted by these theorists' arguments and the facts. Thus their exaggeration of an essentially valid observation (the necessity and great importance of leadership) into an unwarranted conclusion (the impossibility of democracy) caused the valid and stimulating parts of their work to be ignored by most political scientists. The theorists have often been guilty of even greater sins than exaggeration. Their ideas have sometimes been contradictory, their concepts poorly defined, and the claims made for the significance of their work unnecessarily grandiose. Nor have they shown any desire to test their ideas by applying them to concrete facts.

What is clearly needed in such a situation is the fruitful blending of the empirical researcher's devotion to facts with the theorist's urge to generalize and interpret them. The present hiatus between the theory and empirical research pertaining to political decision-makers must be reduced if further progress is to be made.

Social Backgrounds and Decision-Making

Certainly the principal reason for the political scientists' interest in social backgrounds has been to obtain thereby a better understanding of the behavior of decision-makers in office and a greater insight into why they decide as they do. It was hoped that the consideration of the human factors would rescue political science from legalistic formalism. Taken as a whole, the research done on social backgrounds has not lived up to these expectations. Sometimes a new formalism of facts and figures has merely replaced the older legalism. Studies like Bailey's *Congress Makes A Law* and Truman's *The Governmental Process* show that social background data, when used in conjunction with more conventional material and approaches, can help explain why important decisions are made.[4] But these studies are the brilliant exceptions rather than the rule. This is the field in the author's estimation, toward which most of the future efforts of scholars should be directed.

Implications for Public Policy

It may be presumptuous after the previous remarks to suggest that the find-ings of this study have implications for public policy in America. None the less the findings on the recruitment of decision-makers do seem to have such policy implications.

The success of a political democracy, no less than the success of any other political system, depends upon the development of competent leadership. The relatively small group of political decision-makers in the United States carry on the day to day business of government. Perhaps even more important, they influence very heavily the quality of American public opinion. Public opinion is not, in Justice Holmes' words, "a brooding omnipotence in the sky" which possesses a separate existence from leadership. Rather the American people choose between alternatives of policy and personnel. If the alternatives are good ones, public opinion can be wise. If the alternatives are ill-conceived, public opinion must be unsatisfactory. And these alternatives are provided by America's political leaders—official decision-makers, party and pressure group leaders, the press. The competence with which our decision-makers perform these tasks is now in dispute and always will be. Very probably they perform their jobs a good deal more adequately than most Americans realize. Yet no one would deny that there is room for improvement. How can our limited insight into the recruitment of official decision-makers help us secure more able and competent leadership in the future? Our previous analysis suggests that several courses of action which would probably better the caliber of our decision-makers are open to us.

First, every effort might be made to reduce the existing blocks to political achievement and to broaden the base of recruitment. Higher salaries for public officials, more adequate methods of financing political campaigns, and efforts to make politics a more appealing career are often suggested as means to that end; and, if put into effect, they would no doubt help. But perhaps an even greater result would be obtained from efforts to encourage over-all social mobility, to make competition for the social positions from which decision-makers are usually selected more nearly equal. A greater equalization of educa-tional opportunity, the elimination of discrimination against women, Negroes, and other minority groups would contribute to this. There are many reasons why these measures seem desirable to democrats, yet one reason which is often overlooked is that these policies would make the opportunities to compete for top-level public office more nearly equal. Under such conditions less native talent would be wasted and recruitment very probably would be more efficient than it is now.

These proposals are intended only to suggest a few ways in which the re-cruitment of political decision-makers can be altered once it is realized that leadership selection is going on throughout America every day and is not just confined to primaries and elections. But, it can be argued, this list of suggested policies is meaningless and sterile. It is rather like beginning an argument by saying, "If men were angels." The suggested policies are based upon the assumption that the desirable course is to make the recruitment process more truly competitive, yet many feel that American society is becoming more stratified and less competitive every day. While the evidence on this point is by no means conclusive, it may be true. Americans may well have to reconcile themselves to an even less competitive system of political recruitment in future years. If this should happen, a wise public policy would take advantage of the disadvantages of this situation. Under such conditions political opportunities would be more unequal than they are today and, very probably, determined far earlier in life. This situation has one advantage: it is possible to provide special training for those who are likely to be the next generation's political leaders. Under these circumstances this opportunity should be exploited. There are great risks involved in pursuing such a policy: a closed group of decision-makers might be formed which would have little contact with the remainder of the population. But this danger can be avoided, as the experience of Great Britain demonstrates clearly.

Thus it seems that the United States might improve the caliber of its decision-makers in two different ways. Under the first alternative Americans would attempt to judge political competence by actual performance under conditions of equal competition. Under the second system the United States would try to ensure that its future political leaders were competent through special education and training. Most Americans, including the author, would instinctively prefer the first of these two alternatives; yet in an age which seems to be characterized by increasing class distinctions, the advantages of the second should not be ignored. The present American system which combines quite substantial inequalities in opportunities with no special training for the small group from which most of the leaders of the nation are chosen, combines the disadvantages, rather than the advantages, of both of the other alternatives. In the long run, it is for all Americans to decide which course shall be followed.

Sources for Tables

1. Anderson, H. D.: "Educational and Occupational Attainments of Our National Rulers," *Scientific Monthly* 40:516 (1935); Bendix, R.: *Higher Civil Servants in American Society*. (University of Colorado Studies, Series in Sociology #1), Boulder, University of Colorado Press, 1949, p. 26; Matthews, D. R.: *United States Senators: A Study of the Recruitment of Political Leaders*. Unpublished Ph.D. dissertation, Princeton University, 1953, p. 70; McKinney, M.: "The Personnel of the 77th Congress," *American Political Science Review* 36:74 (1942); Sogge, T. M.: "Industrial Classes in the United States in 1930," *Journal of the American Statistical Association* 28:199–203 (1933). The data from the Anderson, Bendix, and McKinney studies were reclassified by the present author into Sogge's categories. For the criteria of inclusion see A. H. Hanson: "Industrial Class Alignments in the United States," *Journal of the American Statistical Association* 17:417–425 (1920).
2. McCarran, N.: *Negro Congressmen: 1869–1950*. Typewritten manuscript. Legislative Reference Service, Library of Congress, February 13, 1950.
3. Matthews, *op cit.*, p. 67; McKinney, *op. cit.*, p. 68; Haynes, G.: "Senate New Style," *Atlantic Monthly* 134:253 (1924); Haynes, G.: *The Senate of the United States*. Boston, Houghton Mifflin Co., 1938, Vol. 2, p. 1044; Haynes, G.: *The Election of Senators*. Henry Holt and Co., 1906, Ch. 4; Haynes, G.: "The Changing Senate," *North American Review* 200:222–234 (1914).
4. Poll conducted by Representative Leroy Johnson and published in *Look Magazine*, May 23, 1950, p. 116; *Statistical Abstract of the United States,* 1950, p. 17.
5. McKinney, *op. cit.*, p. 69; McKinney, M.: "Religion and Elections," *Public Opinion Quarterly* 8:111 (1944); Matthews, *op. cit.*, p. 77; Williams, L. J.: *Religious Affiliations Expressed by Members of the 81st Congress*. Typewritten manuscript. Legislative Reference Service, Library of Congress, March 31, 1949; *The World Almanac, 1951*, p. 481.
6. Ewing, Cortez E. M.: *The Judges of the Supreme Court, 1789–1937*. Minneapolis, University of Minnesota Press, 1938, p. 79; Anderson, *op. cit.*, p. 512; Bendix, *op. cit.*, p. 32; Matthews, *op. cit.*, p. 88; McKinney, "The Personnel of the 77th Congress," p. 70; Perkins, J. A.: "American Governors, 1930 to 1940," *National Municipal Review* 29:180 (1940); Lange, H. B., Jr.: "They Legislate for Missouri," *Annals* 195:40–41 (1938); U. S. Federal Security Agency, Office of Education, *Biennial Survey of Education, 1938–40,* Vol. 2, p. 41.
7. Anderson, *op. cit.*, p. 514; Matthews, *op. cit.*, p. 117; Williams, L. J.: *Occupational Classification of the Congress of the United States, 1931–1951*. Typewritten manuscript. Legislative Reference Service, Library of Congress, 1950; Perkins, *op. cit.*, p. 180; Hyneman, C. S.: "Who Makes Our Laws?" *Political Science Quarterly* 55:557 (1940); Moore, W. E.: *Industrial Relations and*

the Social Order. Revised edition. New York, The Macmillan Co., 1951, p. 579.

8. Rice, S.: Farmers and Workers in American Politics. (Columbia Studies in History, Economics, and Public Law), New York, Columbia University Press, 1924, pp. 198, 203.
9. Matthews, op. cit., p. 281.
10. Laski, H. J.: "The Personnel of the English Cabinet, 1801–1924," American Political Science Review 22:12–31 (1928); Guttsman, W. L.: "The Changing Social Structure of the British Political Elite, 1886–1935," British Journal of Sociology 2:125 (1951).
11. Guttsman, op. cit., pp. 126, 131; Laski, op. cit., p. 20; Ross, J. F. S.: Parliamentary Representation (London, Eyre and Spottiswoode, 1948, revised edition), pp. 46, 57.
12. Ross, op. cit., pp. 251, 253, 256, 273, 269.
13. Knight, M.: The German Executive. (Hoover Institute Studies, Series B, #4), Stanford, Stanford University Press, 1952, p. 33.
14. Ibid., p. 41.

Footnotes to the Study

IIIIIIIIIIIIIIIIIIIIIIIIIIIIIIIIIIIIIIIIIIIIIIIIIIIIIIIIIIIIIIIIIIIIIIIIIIIIIIIIIIIIIIIIIIIIIIIIIIIIIIIIIIIIIIIIIIIIIIIIIIIIIIIIIIIIIIIIIIIIIIIIIIIIIII

Chapter One

1. Truman, D.: *The Governmental Process* (New York, Alfred A. Knopf, Inc., 1951), p. 262.
2. *Ibid.*, p. 332.
3. Hamilton, Alexander, James Madison, and John Jay: *The Federalist*, No. 10. Modern Library Edition (New York, Random House, 1937), p. 56. It was the recognition of this same fact that led Plato, in the construction of his ideal city in *The Republic*, Book III, to propose the abolition of the private interests of the ruling class by means of communism of wives, children, and property. While other theorists have considered this solution either impractical or undesirable, virtually all great political thinkers have recognized that rulers have personal interests and that these may at times conflict with the public interest. How to ensure the primacy of the latter has been a major concern of political theory at all times.
4. Cf. W. Lippman, *Public Opinion* (New York, The Macmillan Co., 1922) for an early discussion of this phenomenon. See also H. Cantril, *The "Why" of Man's Experience* (New York, The Macmillan Co., 1950); and T. M. Newcomb, *Social Psychology* (New York, The Dryden Press, Inc., 1950), Ch. 6. The example used in the text is suggested by Newcomb, p. 74.
5. The following discussion draws upon a number of sources. For the view that the legislator's "conscience" is likely to be a product of his life experiences see Truman, *op. cit.*, p. 339; and Inter-university Seminar on Political Behavior, "Research in Political Behavior," *American Political Science Review* 46:102 (1952). Moreover, legislators say that their conscience is an important factor in determining their vote. See L. E. Gleek, "96 Congressmen Make Up Their Minds," *Public Opinion Quarterly* 4:3–24 (1940); P. Douglas, "A Senator's Vote: A Searching of the Soul," *The New York Times Magazine*, April 30, 1950, pp. 9 ff. Empirical evidence is slight for the statement that the legislator's personal preference influences what he thinks public opinion is, but see K. Svalastoga, "Notes on Leaders' Estimate of Public Opinion," *Public Opinion Quarterly* 14:767–8 (1950–51); and W. Buchanan, *County Chairmen as Election Forecasters* (Mississippi State College Social Science Studies, Government Series, No. 5, 1952). For the influence of the legislator's past experience on his accessibility to political interest groups see Truman, *op. cit.*, pp. 331–351.
6. Bailey, S. K.: *Congress Makes A Law* (New York, Columbia University Press, 1950), p. 190.
7. Cf. The National Opinion Research Center, *The Public Looks At Politics and the Politician*, Report No. 20 (March, 1944).
8. White, W. S.: "An Audit of the Business Man's Government," *The New York Times Magazine*, May 17, 1953, p. 11. On the same subject see A. A. Berle, Jr., "Businessmen in Government: The New Administration," *The Reporter*,

February 3, 1953, pp. 8–12; and C. Phillips, "The Business Invasion of Washington," *Harper's Magazine* 207:58–63 (1953).

Chapter Two

1. Lynd, Robert: *Knowledge For What?* (Princeton, Princeton University Press, 1946), p. 183. For some recent discussions of the role of theory in empirical research see R. K. Merton, *Social Theory and Social Structure* (Glencoe, Ill., The Free Press, 1949), Introduction; O. Garceau, "Research in the Political Process," *American Political Science Review* 45:69–85 (1951); A. Degrazia (ed.), "Four Essays on the Relation of Political Theory to Research," *Journal of Politics* 13:35–99 (1951); D. Easton, *The Political System* (New York, Alfred A. Knopf, Inc., 1953).
2. Mosca, G.: *The Ruling Class*, edited by A. Livingston and translated by H. D. Kahn (New York, McGraw-Hill Book Co., 1939), p. 50.
3. *Ibid.*, p. 53.
4. *Ibid.*, p. 70.
5. Parsons, T.: "An Analytical Approach to the Theory of Stratification," *Essays In Sociological Theory* (Glencoe, Ill., The Free Press, 1947), Ch. 7. See also K. Davis, "A Conceptual Analysis of Stratification," *American Sociological Review* 7:309–321 (1942); K. Davis and W. E. Moore, "Some Principles of Stratification," *ibid.* 10:242–249 (1945). For a brief summary of the vast literature on American stratification see R. M. Williams, Jr., *American Society* (New York, Alfred A. Knopf, Inc., 1951), Ch. 5, and the works cited therein.
6. Williams, *op. cit.*, p. 79.
7. This discussion of caste and class follows that in Davis and Moore, *op. cit.*
8. For evidence that this is true in America see P. C. Hatt and C. North, "Jobs and Occupations: A Popular Evaluation," *Opinion News* 9:3–13 (September 1, 1947). According to this study six of the ten most highly valued occupations were public offices. This prestige does not always transfer to the normal incumbents of the offices, however, as the low prestige of the "politician" in America testifies.
9. Cf. R. M. MacIver, *The Web of Government* (New York, The Macmillan Co., 1948), Ch. 2; H. D. Lasswell and A. Kaplan, *Power and Society* (New Haven, Yale University Press, 1950), p. 154; R. Michels, "Authority," *Encyclopaedia of the Social Sciences* (New York, The Macmillan Co., 1930), Vol. 2, p. 320.
10. Russell, B.: *Power, A New Social Analysis* (New York, W. W. Norton and Co., 1938), pp. 17–18.
11. Timasheff, N. S.: *An Introduction to the Sociology of Law* (Cambridge, Harvard University Press, 1939), Ch. 8.
12. Merriam, Charles: *Political Power; Its Composition and Incidence* (New York, McGraw-Hill Book Co., 1934), p. 263.
13. Pareto, Vilfredo: *The Mind and Society*, edited and translated by A. Livingston (New York, Harcourt, Brace and Co., 1935), 4 vol. See especially para. 889 ff., 991 ff., 2178 ff.
14. Lasswell, H.: *Power and Personality* (New York, W. W. Norton and Co., Inc., 1948), p. 22. Italics in the original have been omitted. See also his *Psychopathology and Politics* (Chicago, University of Chicago Press, 1930), *passim*.
15. Whyte, W. F.: "Social Organization of the Slums," *American Sociological Review* 8:34–39 (1943). See also his *Street Corner Society* (Chicago, University of Chicago Press, 1943), Part IV.
16. Cf. Merton, *op. cit.*, p. 5 ff.

17. Burnham, J.: *The Managerial Revolution* (New York, The John Day Co., 1941), pp. 59, 28, 59.
18. *Ibid.*, p. 72.
19. *Ibid.*, pp. 150, 259–260.
20. The argument summarized below is found in Karl Mannheim, *Man and Society in an Age of Reconstruction* (New York, Harcourt, Brace and Co., 1950, reprint), especially at pp. 53–56. His suggested countermeasures for the anti-democratic consequences of the industrial revolution are presented at *ibid.*, pp. 74, 113–4, 364–5; and in *Freedom, Power and Democratic Planning* (New York, Oxford University Press, 1950), passim.
21. Mannheim, *Man and Society in an Age of Reconstruction*, p. 63.
22. Pareto, *op. cit.*, para. 2178, 2313, 2231, 2329 ff.
23. Lasswell, H. D.: "The Garrison State and Specialists on Violence," in *The Analysis of Political Behavior* (London, Routledge, Kegan Paul, Ltd., 1948, first published, 1941), pp. 146–157; and Lasswell, H. D., D. Lerner, and C. E. Rothwell: *The Comparative Study of Elites*, Hoover Institute Studies, Series B., No. 1 (Stanford, Stanford University Press, 1952). Cf. H. D. Lasswell, *The World Revolution of Our Time*, Hoover Institute Studies, Series A, No. 1 (Stanford, Stanford University Press, 1951), p. 4 ff., for a brief explanation of "developmental constructs."
24. Seligman, L. G.: "The Study of Political Leadership," *American Political Science Review*, 44:907 (1950).
25. The following paragraph draws heavily upon C. W. Cassinelli, "The Law of Oligarchy," *American Political Science Review*, 47:781 (1953).
26. Herring, E. P.: *Presidential Leadership* (New York, Farrar and Rinehart, Inc., 1940), pp. 18–19.
27. Michels, R.: *Political Parties: A Sociological Study of the Oligarchical Tendencies of Modern Democracy*, translated by E. and C. Paul (Glencoe, Ill., The Free Press, 1949, reprint), p. 164. Emphasis added.
28. Friedrich, C. J.: *Constitutional Government and Politics* (New York, Harper and Brothers, 1937), pp. 16–18.

Chapter Three

1. Garceau, *op. cit.*, p. 77.
2. Merriam, Charles: *Four American Party Leaders* (New York, The Macmillan Co., 1926); Salter, J. T.: *Boss Rule: Portraits in City Politics* (New York, The Macmillan Co., 1935); and Lasswell, *Psychopathology and Politics*.
3. Garceau, *op. cit.*, p. 77.
4. Cf. M. Parten, *Surveys, Polls and Samples* (New York, Harper and Brothers, 1950), pp. 94–96, for a good discussion of mail questionnaires.
5. A list of biographical directories for the various regions may be found in Lasswell, Lerner, and Rothwell, *op. cit.*, pp. 66–72. This book contains the only bibliography in the field.
6. Cf. *Biography Index* (New York, H. W. Wilson Co., 1946–) for a highly useful index of American biography appearing in books and periodicals.
7. Cf. R. Williams, *op. cit.*, Ch. 5, and the works cited therein, as well as the large number of community studies such as R. S. and H. M. Lynd, *Middletown* (New York, Harcourt, Brace and Co., 1929) and *Middletown in Transition* (New York, Harcourt, Brace and Co., 1937); W. L. Warner and P. S. Lunt, *The Social Life of a Modern Community* (New Haven, Yale University Press, 1941); W. L. Warner and Associates, *Democracy in Jonesville* (New York, Harper and Brothers, 1949); A. B. Hollingshead, *Elmtown's Youth* (New York, John Wiley and Sons, Inc., 1949); A. Davis, B. B. and M. R. Gardner, *Deep South* (Chicago, University of Chicago Press, 1941).

8. Zink, H.: *City Bosses in the United States* (Durham, N.C., Duke University Press, 1930), p. 7.
9. The phrase is that of S. Lubell, *The Future of American Politics* (New York, Harper and Brothers, 1951). See pp. 67 ff. for an account of the "coming of age" of the Italian-American group in Rhode Island. Lubell's entire book should be consulted by anyone interested in the role of ethnic groups in American politics.
10. McKinney, M.: "Religion and Elections," *Public Opinion Quarterly* 8:113 (1944).
11. Anderson, H. D.: "Educational and Occupational Attainments of Our National Rulers," *Scientific Monthly* 40:512 (1935), Table II.
12. Cf. Hollingshead, *op. cit.*, *passim*; E. Sibley, "Some Demographic Clues to Stratification," in L. Wilson and W. Kolb (eds.), *Sociological Analysis* (New York, Harcourt, Brace and Co., 1949), pp. 642–650.
13. Anderson, *op. cit.*, p. 514, Table III.
14. Brown, E. L.: *Lawyers, Law Schools and the Public Service* (New York, Russell Sage Foundation, 1948), p. 17. See also J. B. Mason, "The Trend: Lawyers in the 71st and 75th Congress," *Rocky Mountain Law Review* 10:43–52 (1937); W. Miller "American Lawyers in Business and Politics," *Yale Law Review* 60:66–76 (1951).
15. Lasswell, H. D., and M. S. McDougal: "Legal Education and Public Policy," in Lasswell, *The Analysis of Political Behavior* (London, Routledge, Kegan Paul, Ltd., 1948), p. 27.
16. Barber, B.: *"Mass Apathy" and Voluntary Social Participation in the United States*, Unpublished Ph.D. dissertation (Harvard, 1948), p. 118.
17. Weber, M.: "Politics as a Vocation," in *From Max Weber: Essays in Sociology*, H. H. Gerth and C. W. Mills, editors and translators (New York, Oxford University Press, Inc., 1946), p. 85.
18. It is standard practice for a candidate for elective office to pay at least part of his personal campaign expenses. See D. D. McKean, *Party and Pressure Politics* (Boston, Houghton Mifflin Co., 1949), p. 345. For the more important offices this contribution may be quite substantial. Senator Lehman (D, N.Y.) invested $21,000 in his campaign for re-election in 1950. See S. K. Bailey and H. D. Samuels, *Congress at Work* (New York, Henry Holt and Co., Inc., 1952), p. 23; C. Phillips, "The High Cost of Our Low-Paid Congress," *The New York Times Magazine*, February 24, 1952, estimates that a Congressman must have an income of $3,000 per year beyond his Congressional salary in order to avoid going into debt.
19. Several community studies have suggested that in local politics the members of the highest ranking class are not particularly active in politics but that the upwardly mobile "strivers" ranking below them are. Upper-class control is maintained through their control of these subordinates. Cf. Warner, *Democracy in Jonesville*, Ch. 13, and the other community studies cited above in note 7.
20. Lehman, H. C.: *Age and Achievement* (Princeton, Princeton University Press, 1953), pp. 163–4; Ewing, C. A. M.: *The Judges of the Supreme Court* (Minneapolis, University of Minnesota Press, 1938), p. 69, Figure 10; Bendix, R.: *Higher Civil Servants in American Society*, University of Colorado Studies, Series in Sociology, No. 1 (Boulder, University of Colorado Press, 1949), p. 23; McKinney, M.: "The Personnel of the 77th Congress," *American Political Science Review* 36:68 (1942).
21. Women's Division, Republican National Committee: *Women in the Public Service*. Mimeographed, 1953. This annual survey may be obtained from the Republican National Committee.
22. Smith, M., and M. L. Brockway: "Mobility of American Congressmen,"

Sociology and Social Research 24:511–525 (1940); Matthews, D. R., *United States Senators: A Study of the Recruitment of Political Leaders,* Unpublished Ph.D. dissertation (Princeton University, 1952), p. 78 ff.; Bendix *op. cit.,* p. 22 ff.
3. Allport, F. H.: *Social Psychology* (Boston, Houghton Mifflin Co., 1924), pp. 422–423.
4. Bogardus, E. S.: *Fundamentals of Social Psychology* (New York, Appleton-Century-Crofts, Inc., 1942), Ch. 12.
5. Stogdill, R. M.: "Personal Factors Associated with Leadership: A Survey of the Literature," *Journal of Psychology* 25:64 (1948).
6. Gibb, C.: "The Principles and Traits of Leadership," *Journal of Abnormal and Social Psychology* 42:283 (1947).
7. Stogdill, *op. cit.,* p. 64.
8. Merriam, Charles: *Political Power* (New York, McGraw-Hill Book Co., 1934), pp. 40–46.
9. Salter, J. T.: "The Politician and the Voter," Ch. 3, in E. B. Logan (ed.), *The American Political Scene* (New York, Harper and Brothers, 1936), p. 111. See also Salter, *Boss Rule,* p. 10.
10. See J. B. McConaughy, "Certain Personality Factors of State Legislators in South Carolina," *American Political Science Review* 44:897–903 (1950) for one attempt to study systematically the personality characteristics of public officials.
11. Gouldner, A. W.: *Studies in Leadership* (New York, Harper and Brothers, 1950), pp. 24–25. I have drawn upon Gouldner's entire introductory essay in writing this paragraph.
12. The following discussion is based upon Lasswell, *Power and Personality,* especially pp. 44–54, 40; *Psychopathology and Politics,* especially pp. 76–77, 151–152.
13. Lasswell, *Psychopathology and Politics,* pp. 78–79. Copyrighted by and used with the permission of the University of Chicago.
14. *Ibid.,* pp. 125–126. Copyrighted by and used with the permission of the University of Chicago.
15. Lasswell, *Power and Personality,* p. 62. Copyrighted by and used with the permission of W. W. Norton and Co., Inc.
16. See Lasswell, *Psychopathology and Politics,* Chs. 6–8; and *Power and Personality,* Ch. 4; H. Zink, "A Case Study of a Political Boss," *Psychiatry* 1:527–533 (1938); L. Smith, "Aaron Burr," *Psychoanalytic Quarterly* 12:67–99 (1943); G. M. Gilbert, *The Psychology of Dictatorship* (New York, The Ronald Press Company, 1950); R. K. Merton, "Bureaucratic Structure and Personality," in A. W. Gouldner (ed.), *op. cit.,* pp. 67–79; and H. D. Lasswell, *Politics: Who Gets What, When, How* (New York, McGraw-Hill Book Co., 1936), Ch. 8.
17. Beard, Charles: *An Economic Interpretation of the Constitution of the United States* (New York, The Macmillan Co., 1913).
18. *Ibid.,* p. 149.
19. Rice, Stuart: *Farmers and Workers in American Politics,* Columbia Studies in History, Economics, and Public Law, Vol. CXIII, No. 2 (New York, Columbia University Press, 1924), Ch. VI. The index of cohesion is explained in S. Rice, *Quantitative Methods in Politics* (New York, Alfred A. Knopf, Inc., 1928), Ch. XV.
20. See B. R. Brimhall and A. S. Otis, "Consistency in Congressional Voting," *Journal of Applied Psychology* 32:1–15 (1948); N. L. Gage and B. Shimberg, "Measuring Senatorial 'Progressivism,'" *Journal of Abnormal and Social Psychology* 44:112–117 (1949); and S. P. Huntington, "A Revised Theory of American Politics," *American Political Science Review* 44:669–677 (1950).

41. Lasswell, *Power and Personality*, pp. 63 ff., 101 ff.; Truman, *op. cit.*, pp. 343–350.

Chapter Four

1. Guttsman, W. L.: "The Changing Social Structure of the British Political Elite," *British Journal of Sociology* 2:133–4 (1951).
2. Cf. K. H. Abshagen, *Kings, Lords and Gentlemen: Influence and Power of the English Upper Classes* (London, William Heinemann, Ltd., 1939).
3. Laski, H. J.: "The Personnel of the English Cabinet, 1901–1924," *American Political Science Review* 22:23 (1928).
4. Ross, J. F. S.: *Parliamentary Representation* (London, Eyre and Spottis-woode, 1948, revised edition), pp. 52, 57, 74. The reader who desires more information on the background of Members of Parliament is referred to this standard work. For data on earlier periods see H. R. Greaves, "Personal Origins and Interrelations of the Houses of Parliament (Since 1832)," *Economica* 9:173–184 (1929); and J. A. Thomas, *The House of Commons, 1832–1901* (Cardiff, University of Wales Press, 1937). More recent material on parliamentary candidates may be found in R. B. McCallum and A. Readman, *The British General Election of 1945* (London, Oxford University Press, 1947); H. G. Nicholas, *The British General Election of 1950* (London, Macmillan and Co., Inc., 1951); and D. E. Butler, *The British General Election of 1951* (London, Macmillan and Co., Inc., 1952).
5. While 42% of the Parliamentary Labor Party are listed as "workers," 32% are also listed as trade-union officials. If one assumes that all the trade-union officials are listed in the worker category, this means that only 10% of the Parliamentary Labor Party are workers without also being union leaders; see Ross, *op. cit.*, p. 271. In the election the Labor Party had 108 workers as candidates. Of these, 57 were full-time trade-union officials. See Butler, *op. cit.*, p. 40.
6. Space does not permit a discussion of trends in social background of civil servants. On this see J. D. Kingsley, *Representative Bureaucracy* (Yellow Springs, Ohio, The Antioch Press, 1944); H. E. Dale, *The Higher Civil Service of Great Britain* (London, Oxford University Press, 1941); and R. T. Nightingdale, "The Personnel of the British Foreign Office and Diplomatic Service, 1851–1929," *American Political Science Review* 24:310–331 (1930).
7. Knight, M.: *The German Executive, 1890–1933*, Hoover Institute Studies, Series B, No. 4 (Stanford, Stanford University Press, 1952).
8. *Ibid.*, pp. vi–vii.
9. *Ibid.*, p. iii.
10. *Ibid.*, p. 49.
11. Lerner, D., with I. de Sola Pool and G. K. Schueller: *The Nazi Elite*, Hoover Institute Studies, Series B, No. 3 (Stanford, Stanford University Press, 1951). For a somewhat different analysis see H. Gerth, "The Nazi Party: Its Leadership and Composition," *American Journal of Sociology* 45:517–541 (1940).
12. Cf. *ibid.* For examples of tables constructed on the basis of highly incomplete data see Tables 11, 12, 28, 29, 34, 36, 37, etc. It is extremely poor sampling technique to assume that the *Don't Know* or *No Data* cases distribute themselves in the same fashion as those cases for which data is known. Also see p. 30 ff., for a case in which the authors assumed that there was a systematic suppression of facts in the *Fuhrerlexicon*. If this assumption is correct in this case, it is correct in other cases as well.
13. *Ibid.*, p. 26.
14. *Ibid.*, pp. 30–33. If the unemployment of intellectuals leads to their "aliena

tion," then it should follow that the intellectuals who became Nazi leaders were more often unemployed during the post-war period than the intellectuals who did not become Nazis. No attempt has ever been made to establish this point.

5. *Ibid.*, p. 84.
6. *Ibid.*, Appendix, pp. 98–9.
7. Schueller, G. K.: *The Politburo*, Hoover Institute Studies, Series B, No. 2 (Stanford, Stanford University Press, 1951). See also J. B. Moore, Jr., "The Communist Party of the Soviet Union: 1928–1944. A Study in Elite Formation and Function," *American Sociological Review* 9:267–278 (1944).
8. Schueller, *op. cit.*, p. 33.
9. *Ibid.*, p. 36.
10. *Ibid.*, p. 32.
11. No better example exists of the "routinization of charisma," Cf. Max Weber, *The Theory of Social and Economic Organization* (New York, Oxford University Press, Inc., 1947), Part III, Section V, p. 363 ff.
12. Inkeles, A.: "Social Stratification and Mobility in the Soviet Union," *American Sociological Review* 15:465–479 (1950).
13. Cf. D. Lerner, "The Role of Brains in the Total State," *Commentary* 16:167–173 (1953); and K. Mannheim, *Ideology and Utopia* (New York, Harcourt, Brace and Co., 1949).

Chapter Five

1. Laski, H. J.: *Democracy in Crisis* (Chapel Hill, N. C., University of North Carolina Press, 1933), p. 80.
2. In addition to the works already cited the reader interested in administrators should consult A. MacMahon and J. D. Millett, *Federal Administrators* (New York, Columbia University Press, 1939); E. P. Herring, *Federal Commissioners*, (Cambridge, Harvard University Press, 1938); and J. L. McCamy, *The Administration of American Foreign Affairs* (New York, A. A. Knopf, Inc., 1950), Chs. 4, 8. For Congressmen, *Congressional Quarterly Almanac* (Washington, Congressional Quarterly News Features, 1945–) should be consulted. For state legislators see W. B. Graves (ed.), "Our State Legislators," *Annals* 195: entire issue (1938). For state governors see A. F. MacDonald, "American Governors 1900–1910," *National Municipal Review* 16:715–719 (1927); S. R. Soloman, "American Governors since 1915," *National Municipal Review* 20:152–158 (1931); J. A. Perkins, "American Governors, 1930 to 1940," *National Municipal Review* 29:178–184 (1940). For party politicians see W. S. Sayre, "Personnel of Republican and Democratic National Committees," *American Political Science Review* 26:360–363 (1932); and S. Forthal, *Cogwheels of Democracy: A Study of the Precinct Captain* (New York, William-Frederick Press, 1946).
3. Hyneman, C. S.: "Who Makes Our Laws?," *Political Science Quarterly* 55:557 (1940). Emphasis added.
4. Bailey, *op. cit.*, Ch. 10; Truman, *op. cit.*, Ch. 11.

DOUBLEDAY SHORT STUDIES IN POLITICAL SCIENCE
Consulting Editor
Richard C. Snyder
Associate Professor of Politics, Princeton University

Spring, 1954

The Revolution in American Foreign Policy, 1945–1954
By William G. Carleton, Professor of Political Science and Head Professor of the Social Sciences, University of Florida

Political Community at the International Level: Problems of Definition and Measurement
By Karl W. Deutsch, Professor of History and Political Science, Massachusetts Institute of Technology

France: Keystone of Western Defense
By Edgar S. Furniss, Jr., Assistant Professor of Politics, Princeton University

The Problem of Internal Security in Great Britain, 1948–1953
By H. H. Wilson, Associate Professor of Politics, Princeton University and Harvey Glickman, Fellow, Harvard University

Germany: Dilemma for American Foreign Policy
By Otto Butz, Visiting Research Scholar, Center of International Studies, Princeton University

The Role of the Military in American Foreign Policy
By Burton M. Sapin, Research Assistant, Foreign Policy Analysis Project, Princeton University and Richard C. Snyder, Associate Professor of Politics, Princeton University

Democratic Rights Versus Communist Activity
By Thomas I. Cook, Professor of Political Science, The Johns Hopkins University

The Social Background of Political Decision-Makers
By Donald R. Matthews, Assistant Professor of Government, Smith College

Readings in Game Theory and Political Behavior
By Martin Shubik, Research Associate, Economic Analysis Project, Princeton University

Fall, 1954

The American Vice-Presidency: New Look
By Irving G. Williams, Associate Professor and Chairman, Departments of History and Social Studies, St. John's University

Contemporary International Law: A Balance Sheet
By Quincy Wright, Professor of Political Science, University of Chicago

Law as a Political Instrument
By Victor G. Rosenblum, Assistant Professor of Political Science, University of California, Berkeley

The Political Fate of the Non-Communist Left in Postwar France
By E. Drexel Godfrey, Jr., Assistant Professor of Political Science, Williams College

The Political Process: Executive Bureau—Congressional Committee Relations
By J. Leiper Freeman, Assistant Professor and Research Associate, Graduate School of Education, Harvard University

Agriculture and Politics: A Study in Power
By Robert Engler, Professor of Political Science, Sarah Lawrence College

Studies in Scope and Methods

The Study of Public Administration
By Dwight Waldo, Professor of Political Science, University of California, Berkeley

The Study of Political Theory
By Thomas P. Jenkin, Professor of Political Science and Chairman of the Department, University of California, Los Angeles

The Study of Comparative Government
By Roy C. Macridis, Associate Professor of Political Science, Northwestern University

Problems of Analyzing and Predicting Soviet Behavior
By John S. Reshetar, Jr., Lecturer in Politics, Princeton University

You may enter your subscription for the series now so that you will be sure to receive on approval each study as soon as it is published. The studies will be priced at no more than $1.00. Address COLLEGE DEPARTMENT, Doubleday & Company, Inc., 575 Madison Avenue, New York 22, N.Y.